THE lighted LADY

An imprint of The Lighted Lady LLC
1109 S Park St Ste 504-339, Carrollton, GA 30117
Copyright © 2018 The Lighted Lady LLC

All rights reserved.

ISBN/SKU:9780692081181
ISBN Complete:978-0-692-08118-1

No parts of this publication may be reproduced, stored in a retrieval system, or transmitted in any form or by any means, electronic, mechanical, photocopying, recording, or otherwise, without the prior written permission of the copyright owner.

This book is sold subject to the condition that it shall not, by way of trade or otherwise, be lent, resold, hired out, or otherwise circulated without the publisher's prior consent in any form of binding or cover other than that in which it is published and without a similar condition including this condition being imposed on the subsequent purchaser. Under no circumstances may any part of this book be photocopied for resale.

Cover Design created with Canva.com

Scripture quotations taken from the Amplified® Bible (AMP),
Copyright © 2015 by The Lockman Foundation
Used by permission. www.Lockman.org

Scripture taken from the New King James Version®. Copyright © 1982 by Thomas Nelson. Used by permission. All rights reserved.

Italics, Bold, and Capitalization in Scripture quotations have been added by the author for emphasis.
First Edition: March 2018
Printed in the United States of America

A BEGINNER'S GUIDE TO
FAITH-BASED ACTION PLANNING

SASHA LEDAWN

This book is dedicated to my father, my sunshine, my warrior, and my guardian angel

KENNETH A. THOMAS

Your life and dedication to me will forever ensure that this dreamer will **always** reach for her dreams.

TABLE OF CONTENTS

Chapter 1	Introduction	Chapter 16	Take Thoughts Captive
Chapter 2	Deep Calls Unto Deep	Chapter 17	Go Be Great
Chapter 3	He Weeps With Us	Chapter 18	Stop Wasting Time
Chapter 4	Prayer is Stronger Than You	Chapter 19	Blessed Who Endure
Chapter 5	Reclaim Your Inheritance	Chapter 20	Wait For It
Chapter 6	Guard Your Heart	Chapter 21	Diligence Leads To Abund.
Chapter 7	Rule Your Spirit	Chapter 22	Be A Cheerful Giver
Chapter 8	Don't Come Down	Chapter 23	Always Give Thanks
Chapter 9	Fear is Fake	Chapter 24	Choose Friends Wisely
Chapter 10	He Gives And He Takes	Chapter 25	By Your Spirit
Chapter 11	You're Graced For This	Chapter 26	Faith is Action
Chapter 12	Don't Worry About It	Chapter 27	No Pride Allowed
Chapter 13	Don't Despise Small Beginnings	Chapter 28	Hope Doesn't Disappoint
Chapter 14	Giants Do Fall	Chapter 29	This is My Comfort
Chapter 15	Press equals Progress	Chapter 30	Time to Fish
		Chapter 31	Hallelujah

INTRODUCTION

HELLO &
THANK YOU

Welcome to **ENVISION ME**! First and foremost I want to thank you for investing in this book and in yourself. Your future possibilities in God are astounding and if you could see it all at once it would absolutely take your breath away. The issue that I find and continue to find in the Christian community is at we have trouble **ENVISIONING**. Our daily lives involve trouble and survival, circumstances and tribulation. We see goodness happening all around us but we won't believe that it could possibly happen to us. The waves and waves disappointment and frustrations have deafened our ears and dulled our sight. I understand it, but today is where the table turns. Today is the beginning of a new life and a new you.

Envision Me is simple but revolutionary because it cultivates **a relationship with God** through three simple steps:

STEP 1: READ
We can't talk about vision and skip over one, if not, the most critical tools for establishing and maintaining vision. 2 Timothy 3:16-17 says that *All Scripture is given by inspiration of God, and is profitable for doctrine, for reproof, for correction, for instruction in righteousness, that the man of God may be complete, thoroughly equipped for every good work.* (NKJV). If we want to be complete (whole) and equipped to carry out God's vision then we have to read the infallible, inspirational word of God every single day.

STEP 2: PLAN
Our busy lives are filled with distractions. Day in and day out we are bombarded with things that are vying for our attention. There is just no way to successfully complete what God is telling us to do if we don't plan for it. To have a plan means to be intentional with our time.

STEP 3: WRITE
Write the vision and make it plain on tablets, that he may run who reads it. (Habakkuk 2:2 NKJV) If we want action, progress, and manifestation we have to write it down. Writing is the action word that promotes constant movement. Read, Plan. Live it out and Write it down. It's just that simple!

Now may the God of peace who brought up our Lord Jesus from the dead, that great Shepherd of the sheep, through the blood of the everlasting covenant, make you complete in every good work to do His will, working in you what is well pleasing in His sight, through Jesus Christ, to whom be glory forever and ever. Amen.

Hebrews 13:20-21

GOD, PLEASE CHOOSE SOMEONE ELSE

How many times have you prayed this prayer? I know I have said this to God a lot because I didn't feel like He had the right person in mind for all things great things He spoke to me about. If He told me it was for my pastor or best friend, I would believe him wholeheartedly. I would be in the front row cheering them on. " YOU GOT THIS", I would be screaming at the top of lungs and when times got hard I would be right there with choice words and encouragement. The problem is God didn't call them for this vision he placed on my heart. He called me. I so deeply want to say yes but in my heart is a resounding no. I can't do this. My best friend, yeah, she can do this. My pastor would be perfect for this. He's amazing. That homeless man on the corner, man, God he would be perfect for what you just told me. Why on earth would you choose me for this? God, please choose someone else.

HE CHOSE YOU AND IT WAS ON PURPOSE

Well, to save you some time, God is not going to skip over you like a game of hopscotch. Process it. Believe it. Walk in it. An omnipotent God has spent all that infinite power, limitless knowledge to create you. He knows even the count of hairs on your head. **(Luke 12:7)** He knows, knew, and foreknew you. He knew how you would dress and what foods you would like even before your great, great, great, great, (you get the idea) grandmother even existed. God knows your lineage, heritage, all your weaknesses and shortcomings, strengths and quirks, secret sins and highest hopes. If every second of your life were recorded in a book, God would have already read it. In fact, He would've already written it! (that's good).

God was intentional about creating you. He created the earth, the sun, and He thought, in His masterful mind, even after creating the vast heavens, that it all wouldn't be complete without you. What that means is that you have a reason for being alive right now. You don't deserve a purposeless existence and you weren't created for one.

You have a divine mission and it goes beyond being born, making money, and dying. There is more and YOU have to believe it. This is the part where you have to make a choice. You can't hold on to your will and God's. You have to put all your eggs(your hopes, vision, and plans) in one basket called God and leave them there. Give it to God now. Let go! Release it!

Therefore humble yourselves under the mighty hand of God, that He may exalt you in due time, casting all your care upon Him, for He cares for you. (**1 Peter 5:6-7**)

Humble yourself and accept that you just don't know what is best for you. Submit all you have to Him. Cast it all on him. Cast means to throw so do that. Throw it all to Him. Exhaust all that is in your heart. He can handle it. The question is can you handle the extraordinary life that He has planned for you? If not, get ready. This is the point in your life where everything changes.

THERE IS HEALING IN LETTING GO

RELEASE & RECIEVE

We all have circumstances that we wish we could change. It can be even more painful to know that we have a God that could have prevented it or changed it all but didn't. Unspoken grievances with God and others prevent healing and halts progress. Psalms 147:3 says, *He heals the brokenhearted and binds up their wounds*. He can help you heal but you have to let Him back in.

What has broken your heart?

What do you need to let go of?

FAITH IS ACTION

JAMES 2:14-26

WHAT IS THE VISION FOR MY LIFE?

Vision is a very complicated topic to explain. It has many layers. It's not limited to just one action. It encompasses your purpose, mind, faith, and life. Vision is multidimensional, just as our God. Envisioning is the purpose of this book. If you don't understand it to some degree, it will make it difficult for you to understand the topics presented in this book. Let's take a moment to dissect vision before you begin your journey.

SIGHT DOESN'T DISCRIMINATE

God's Overarching Vision

The broad scope of God's vision for our lives is that everyone be saved. John 3:16-17 says "**For God so loved the world that He gave His only begotten Son, that whoever believes in Him should not perish but have everlasting life. For God did not send His Son into the world to condemn the world, but that the world through Him might be saved,**"(NKJV).

Salvation is the foundational element of faith and the launching point to fulfilling God's vision for our lives. It means to be saved from eternal death. Hell is a real. You may already know that but just in case you don't let me put it to you plainly that without Christ you will go there. There is no wiggle room on this. The good news is that you don't have to go! It is in God's vision for you to go to heaven and experience His goodness here on earth, too. If you wish to be saved, then say the following prayer with me:

God, I am a sinner. I am unclean in your sight and I know that I cannot redeem myself. I acknowledge my need for Salvation and savior. I confess right now that Jesus Christ is Lord of my life. God, I believe that you gave your only begotten son as ransom for me and that you raised Him from the dead that I might be saved. I thank you for caring that much about me. Come into my heart. Change my life. I surrender my life to you and I accept your adoption in to the Kingdom. Amen.

And that's it! You have officially taken your first step into a brand-new life. You won't be going through it alone either. You now have a whole new family ready and willing to walk with you through your life's obstacles. There is also a sweet, yet powerful helper that will always be with you. It's called the Holy Spirit and it will guide you through the truth. It is your seal of redemption. Nothing will ever be able to take that away from you. Ephesians 1:13-14 explains it best. It says, "**In Him you also trusted, after you heard the word of truth, the gospel of your salvation; in whom also, having believed, you were sealed with the Holy Spirit of promise, who is the guarantee of our inheritance until the redemption of the purchased possession, to the praise of His glory.**" You are His and he is yours. Welcome home!

Defining Vision

Vision in its simplest form means sight. It is what you are able to perceive with your eyes. It is the process of taking in information. Sight doesn't discriminate. Whatever your eyes see is what your mind will start to process. Envisioning then becomes not just about controlling what you see, but the processes you use to interpret your vision. Two people can stare at the same painting and find something completely different from it. One could see something beautiful in the painting while the other sees something tragic. Envisioning properly will help you to see the good. It aligns itself with hope, not hopelessness. It will promote peace and disconnect you from disappointment.

WHAT YOU PERCEIVE IS WHAT YOU WILL BELIEVE

Envisioning can be broken down into down into 3 aspects: **Perception, Action, and Reception.**

Perception is how you interpret what you see. What you perceive is what you will believe. What you believe will eventually come out in your behavior. It is important to follow God when it comes to perception because of how powerful it is. God's written word is the best way to guide and guard. It instructs us on earthly and spiritual matters. The word discerns, sharpens, and separates us from using our own logic and preconceived notions. If we flood ourselves with the truth, then we can perceive correctly what is good and bad. Our perception is critical to vision. It is a fundamental foundation of vision. Without the right perception, even the clearest vision will eventually come crashing to the ground.

The second principle of vision is action. Abraham, the father of faith, was told to go to a land that He had never seen(**Genesis 12:1**). His action of packing up and leaving is the application of his faith. As a visionary, you will be challenged to act upon things that the Lord reveals little of. You may have to act on the invisible or even in the realm of impossibility. God's ways are higher than ours and He is limitless. We must apply our word to make sure we have good perception, then we must act on whatever He gives us. Vision requires action. You can't do God's word without doing the work.

The third principle is reception. Reception is the acknowledgment of God and acceptance of His divine will. The journey to vision fulfillment is not on a straight path. There are highs and lows that you will not understand. Many times, you will wonder if you're even anywhere near the high mark, much less pressing toward it (**Philippians 3:14-15**). This is where reception comes in. It is all about receiving and it's an ongoing process. Some days you will have to receive God's peace because you won't understand (**Philippians 4:7**). Some nights you will need God's joy after weeping (**Psalm 30:5**). You will need God and you will have to remain in a place that can receive what He wants to give you through prayer.

Defending Vision

Accomplishing God's vision is our primary purpose. His vision for us is His divine plan. It is His will. It is so important that the enemy will launch attacks against all the principles: Perception, Action, and Reception. It doesn't necessarily have to be in that order either. His fiery arrows will be launched but there are ways to dodge his attacks.

HE WILL PULL ON YOUR FLESH SO THAT YOU TRIP OVER YOUR OWN FEET.

He will attack your perception. Remember that your perception is what you see. Expect things to go opposite of the word that you read, or the vision God gave you. If God said you will prosper, you can expect tribulation to come because of that word (**Mark 4:17**). Many individuals in the faith have given up because they were not ready for the opposition tied to the vision. Don't get caught off guard. Expect hardship. Expect it not to be easy. The race is not given to the swift or strong but to the one who endures to the end(**Matthew 24:13**).

The enemy may try to stop your actions. This one can be tricky because it won't be an external opposition but internal ones. He won't try to stop you from acting but he will try to get you to act on the wrong things. He will send distractions that move you out of purpose. He will send temptations to derail you. He will pull on your flesh so that you trip over your own feet. All these pitfalls involve action, just the wrong ones. Watch out for these. The aim is to get you off course. The further off you go, the less dangerous you will be to the powers and principalities that be (**Ephesians 6:12**).

The best way to avoid attacks on the action is to flee. You must run away from the things that your flesh craves and the persistent easy routes the enemy presents. Don't call that friend or answer the phone if it keeps you from being distracted. Don't go to places that will be difficult for you. Don't watch that television show or listen to that song if it will keep you distracted. You get the point. If it won't inspire the right and righteous action, then it does not require your attention.

AS A BELIEVER AND A VISIONARY, YOU MUST BE SET TO KEEP ACKNOWLEDGING GOD, EVEN THROUGH HARSH AND UNFAIR CIRCUMSTANCES

Satan, the accuser of the brethren, will always attack your reception (**Revelation 12:10**). Reception is how you acknowledge God and accept His will. The enemy wants to sift you (**Luke 22:31**). He wants to see you curse God (**Job 1:11**). He is after your relationship. Be aware of this. He wanted to destroy Job's livelihood. He felt that he could get Job to tear down his relationship with God if he could destroy the things that meant the most to him. He tried it and he will try you.

As a believer and a visionary, you must be set to keep acknowledging God, even through harsh and unfair circumstances. **You must choose God every day**. There are days that you may wish that the cup could pass from you just like Jesus did in the garden of Gethsemane (**Matthew 26:39**). You may hate the options set before you. Keep doing God's will. Keep seeking His face. Keep on praying. In the end, you will be restored just as Job (**Job 42:10**).

IF IT WON'T INSPIRE THE RIGHT AND RIGHTEOUS ACTION, THEN IT DOES NOT REQUIRE YOUR ATTENTION.

Faith-walking ain't easy. It will get difficult but it will also be the most satisfying and rewarding experience you will ever have. Remember the three principles of **Perception**, **Action**, and **Reception** as you pursue everything God has for you. Be sure to encourage yourself every step of the way. Bring a witness that can testify about what God is doing in your life. Learn to confess your sins and your heart. Be obedient to what God tells you and **never, ever, give up!**

WRITE IT DOWN
MAKE IT PLAIN

Describe the vision in 7 words or less.

VISION IS WHERE FAITH MEETS HOPE

Write the vision (in detail).

It doesn't have to be pretty or even complete but whatever God is calling you to do must be written down.

THE VISION TEST

We've written a vision but we need to make sure it is THE vision. Answer these short questions to fine-tune what you've already written down. It will separate a vision from a glorified wishlist. **Circle the either Yes or No.**

Have you submitted this vision to God?	YES	NO
Are you disciplined?	YES	NO
Do you have patience?	YES	NO
Are you thankful?	YES	NO
Are you diligent?	YES	NO
Do you attend church frequently or do you have a spiritual covering?	YES	NO
Do you have hope?	YES	NO
Did you read your bible today?	YES	NO

Examine your answers and write down the good, bad, and the ugly that they reveal. Try to be extremely honest.

I AM BRAVE AND UNAFRAID

≡ JOSHUA 1:9 ≡

DEEP CALLS UNTO DEEP

PSALM 42:7

DEEP CALLS UNTO DEEP

Ecclesiastes 1:17(AMP)
And I set my mind to know [practical] wisdom and to discern [the character of] madness and folly [in which men seem to find satisfaction]; I realized that this too is a futile grasping and chasing after the wind.

John 4:14 (AMP)
But whoever drinks the water that I give him will never be thirsty again. But the water that I give him will become in him a spring of water [satisfying his thirst for God] welling up [continually flowing, bubbling within him] to eternal life."

YOU CAN'T DETERMINE HOW TO FULFILL YOU BECAUSE YOU DIDN'T CREATE YOU.

It hurts. It physically and mentally hurts to not know or understand why you were created. Life almost becomes like various shades of gray. Some days are good and some are bad but overall it's, in one word, mediocre. This feeling isn't subject to circumstances either. You may get that job or house. You might achieve a lot of things that other people dream of but it remains just that: Other people's dreams. One day you will wake up and realize that you've done everything "they" told you and it all seems meaningless. Well, it's because "they" aren't what gives life meaning. God is. You can't determine how to fulfill you because you didn't create you.

I know that pierces your soul a bit but it is the harsh truth that brings up an even more difficult question. What on earth have you been doing with you all this time? Think about that for a moment. Solomon lived a life that most of us would sell our limbs for. Success. Money. Power. Prestige. Fame. He had it all AND regretted it all. In my opinion, he found out two things. The first is that none of the aforementioned things actually mattered. The second is that he wasted the most valuable thing, time. Are you starting to see the whole picture now? God's gift is time no matter if you lived for 1,000 years it would never be enough. Our days are numbered down to the last minute and the beauty of it all is that God has a plan for every second.

This plan, found in **Jeremiah 29:11**, won't leave you dry. It will continually breathe into you. His plan will inspire you and captivate you. It won't leave you unsatisfied like the world does. It will replenish and restore your soul. The well supersedes everything you see before your eyes. Are you scared of going that deep in God? It's alright if you are but don't let it stop you. God is calling you. Deep is calling to the deep (**Psalm 42:7**) The mighty God is asking you to drink from a well that will never run dry.

DEEP CALLS UNTO DEEP

Locate Jeremiah 29:11-13 in your bible. Write the scripture down here except replace your name in every place you see the word "you". Read it OUT LOUD to complete this task.

THE WELL SUPERSEDES EVERYTHING YOU SEE BEFORE YOUR EYES.

What do you need from the well?

PRAYER ACTION PLAN

SCRIPTURE: **DATE:**

PRAYER CHANGES EVERYTHING INCLUDING YOU

PRAYER LIST

- [ ]
- [ ]
- [ ]
- [ ]

PRAISE LIST

- [ ]
- [ ]
- [ ]
- [ ]

PRAYER AND REFLECTION

FAITH ACTION PLAN

WHAT MOUNTAIN ARE WE MOVING TODAY?

RESOURCES

OBSTACLES

WHAT DOES IT PROFIT, MY BRETHREN, IF SOMEONE SAYS HE HAS FAITH BUT DOES NOT HAVE WORKS? JAMES 2:14 (NKJV)

TO-DAY LIST

- [ ]
- [ ]
- [ ]
- [ ]
- [ ]
- [ ]
- [ ]

ACTIONABLE STEPS

1.
2.
3.
4.
5.
6.
7.

THOUGHTS & IDEAS

JOURNAL YOUR HEART

Cast your burden on the Lord, And He shall sustain you;
He shall never permit the righteous to be moved.
Psalm 55:22 (NKJV)

CAST YOUR CARE

JOURNAL YOUR FAITH

"Thus speaks the Lord God of Israel, saying: 'Write in a book for yourself all the words that I have spoken to you.
Jeremiah 30:2 (NKJV)

ENCOURAGE YOURSELF

END-OF-THE-DAY
RECAP & REVIEW

What are your thankful for today?

What battles did you win today?

What lessons did you learn today?

**AND WE KNOW THAT ALL THINGS WORK TOGETHER FOR GOOD TO THOSE WHO LOVE GOD, TO THOSE WHO ARE THE CALLED ACCORDING TO HIS PURPOSE.
ROMANS 8:28 (NKJV)**

What did God say to you today?

HE WEEPS WITH US

JOHN 11:33-35

HE WEEPS WITH US

Job 2:10 (NKJV)
But he said to her, "You speak as one of the foolish women speaks. Shall we indeed accept good from God, and shall we not accept adversity?" In all this Job did not sin with his lips.

Isaiah 53:3 (NKJV)
He is despised and rejected by men,
A Man of sorrows and acquainted with grief.
And we hid, as it were, our faces from Him;
He was despised, and we did not esteem Him.

YOUR PAIN WON'T BE THE END OF YOU.

Few things are more painful than the loss of something you thought you would never lose. The pain is beyond anything ever known. It's excruciating, frustrating, and relentless. The constant rush is what makes the world of loss a lonely one. People don't understand why you act the way you do and sometimes you don't know why either. There is no certain way to endure it and there also seems to be no way of escape.

It would be remiss of me to talk about purpose without talking about pain. The pain is different for all of us, yet we all share them: Failure, Disappointment, Death of a Loved One, Rejection, Betrayal, Abuse. The list goes on. The pain goes on. The impact is relentless as if you're forced to go around the same mountain over and over. God!? Why did you allow this to happen to me? The pressure of it all feels like a curse and you've seen the damage it causes. Some people, even in the faith, never recover. Yet, you will recover. You will not stall, stop, nor perish. Your pain won't be the end of you. It may persist in your heart and torment your mind as an ongoing battle but you will live out your victory.

There is a savior that weeps when you weep. You may think He doesn't understand or care but the truth is He does. He sees you (**Genesis 16:13**). He walked the earth that He made, found your grief, and harbored your sorrows. He was rejected by men thousands of years ago and that same rejection is still our first response to pain. It's hard to accept love from the one we hold responsible for our loss. Don't. Refuse to reject the one who lost it all to gain you. He may not have understood you in heaven but that very same God, Christ the Messiah, The King of Kings, came down to Earth. He experienced the very same gut-wrenching pain. Don't hide your face from Him. Don't despise Him. Acknowledge that He feels your pain and that, even in that same pain, He loves you with reckless abandon. He loves you to death and to life. Embrace your comfort from a broken heart. Embrace your remedy to pain. Embrace your Savior.

HE WEEPS
WITH US

It's time for a moment of realness. What are some painful circumstances that you make you angry at God?

REFUSE TO REJECT THE ONE WHO
LOST IT ALL TO GAIN YOU.

How do you plan to overcome the pain you have experienced? How do you plan to allow God into those places of pain?

PRAYER
ACTION PLAN

SCRIPTURE: **DATE:**

PRAYER CHANGES EVERYTHING INCLUDING YOU

PRAYER LIST   **PRAISE LIST**

- [ ]
- [ ]
- [ ]
- [ ]

PRAYER AND REFLECTION

FAITH
ACTION PLAN

WHAT MOUNTAIN ARE WE MOVING TODAY?

RESOURCES

OBSTACLES

WHAT DOES IT PROFIT, MY BRETHREN, IF SOMEONE SAYS HE HAS FAITH BUT DOES NOT HAVE WORKS? JAMES 2:14 (NKJV)

TO-DAY LIST

- [ ]
- [ ]
- [ ]
- [ ]
- [ ]
- [ ]
- [ ]

ACTIONABLE STEPS

1.
2.
3.
4.
5.
6.
7.

THOUGHTS & IDEAS

JOURNAL YOUR HEART

Cast your burden on the Lord, And He shall sustain you;
He shall never permit the righteous to be moved.
Psalm 55:22 (NKJV)

CAST YOUR CARE

JOURNAL
YOUR FAITH

"Thus speaks the Lord God of Israel, saying: 'Write in a book for yourself all the words that I have spoken to you.
Jeremiah 30:2 (NKJV)

ENCOURAGE YOURSELF

END-OF-THE-DAY RECAP & REVIEW

What are your thankful for today?

What battles did you win today?

What lessons did you learn today?

**AND WE KNOW THAT ALL THINGS WORK TOGETHER FOR GOOD TO THOSE WHO LOVE GOD, TO THOSE WHO ARE THE CALLED ACCORDING TO HIS PURPOSE.
ROMANS 8:28 (NKJV)**

What did God say to you today?

PRAYER

IS STRONGER THAN

YOU

JOHN 5:14-15

PRAYER IS
STRONGER THAN YOU

Luke 18:7-8 (NKJV)
And shall God not avenge His own elect who cry out day and night to Him, though He bears long with them? I tell you that He will avenge them speedily. Nevertheless, when the Son of Man comes, will He really find faith on the earth?

1 John 5:14-15 (NKJV)
Now this is the confidence that we have in Him, that if we ask anything according to His will, He hears us. And if we know that He hears us, whatever we ask, we know that we have the petitions that we have asked of Him.

YOU CAN'T MAKE IT HAPPEN.
BUT THERE IS ONE WHO CAN.

There is more to heaven and earth than what we think we know. Our mind is limited and finite. We could combine all the knowledge of 50,000 doctors, scholars, theologians, and rocket scientists and we still would come up short. Our understanding, conclusively, cannot be the standard of God. God is the standard. If you can reason this out in your mind and grasp the fact that He knows so we don't have to know. He fights so we don't have to fight. He makes a way so that we don't have to. Our role then becomes extremely simple: Love God and love those made in his image (**Matthew 22:40**).

Master this. Don't set your heart to master the world. Master your relationship with the Master. Do this and everything else becomes simple and bearable. Afterall, it's His weight, not yours. He has to do it; not you. He may use you but the result is all Him. In this light, the effort we exert shouldn't be applied to moving mountains and overcoming. It should be applied to moving steadily closer and closer to the one who can. That is the secret to godly success. That's how you become as faithful as the centurion (**Matthew 8:10**) and as relentless as the widow who wanted her land. (**Luke 18:1-8**) Don't waste your effort in making it happen. You can't make it happen, but there is one who can. There is one whose mere word can change your whole life. There is one whose touch can bring healing. There is one whose ear you have and whose voice can silence all the chaos of our lives.

God is the answer to every problem that you will ever have. With Him, even the impossible can be made possible. All you need to do is believe. The ability to succeed is given most to those who fall on their knees.

PRAYER IS
STRONGER THAN YOU

What stops you from praying?

_____
_____
_____
_____
_____
_____
_____
_____

MASTER YOUR RELATIONSHIP WITH THE MASTER.

Write about a victory that you know came from prayer.

_____
_____
_____
_____
_____
_____
_____
_____

PRAYER ACTION PLAN

SCRIPTURE: **DATE:**

PRAYER IS POWERFUL

PRAYER LIST
- [ ]
- [ ]
- [ ]
- [ ]

PRAISE LIST
- [ ]
- [ ]
- [ ]
- [ ]

PRAYER AND REFLECTION

FAITH
ACTION PLAN

WHAT MOUNTAIN ARE WE MOVING TODAY?

RESOURCES

OBSTACLES

WHAT DOES IT PROFIT, MY BRETHREN, IF SOMEONE SAYS HE HAS FAITH BUT DOES NOT HAVE WORKS? JAMES 2:14 (NKJV)

TO-DAY LIST
- [ ]
- [ ]
- [ ]
- [ ]
- [ ]
- [ ]
- [ ]

ACTIONABLE STEPS
1.
2.
3.
4.
5.
6.
7.

THOUGHTS & IDEAS

JOURNAL YOUR HEART

Cast your burden on the Lord, And He shall sustain you;
He shall never permit the righteous to be moved.
Psalm 55:22 (NKJV)

CAST YOUR CARE

JOURNAL YOUR FAITH

"Thus speaks the Lord God of Israel, saying: 'Write in a book for yourself all the words that I have spoken to you.
Jeremiah 30:2 (NKJV)

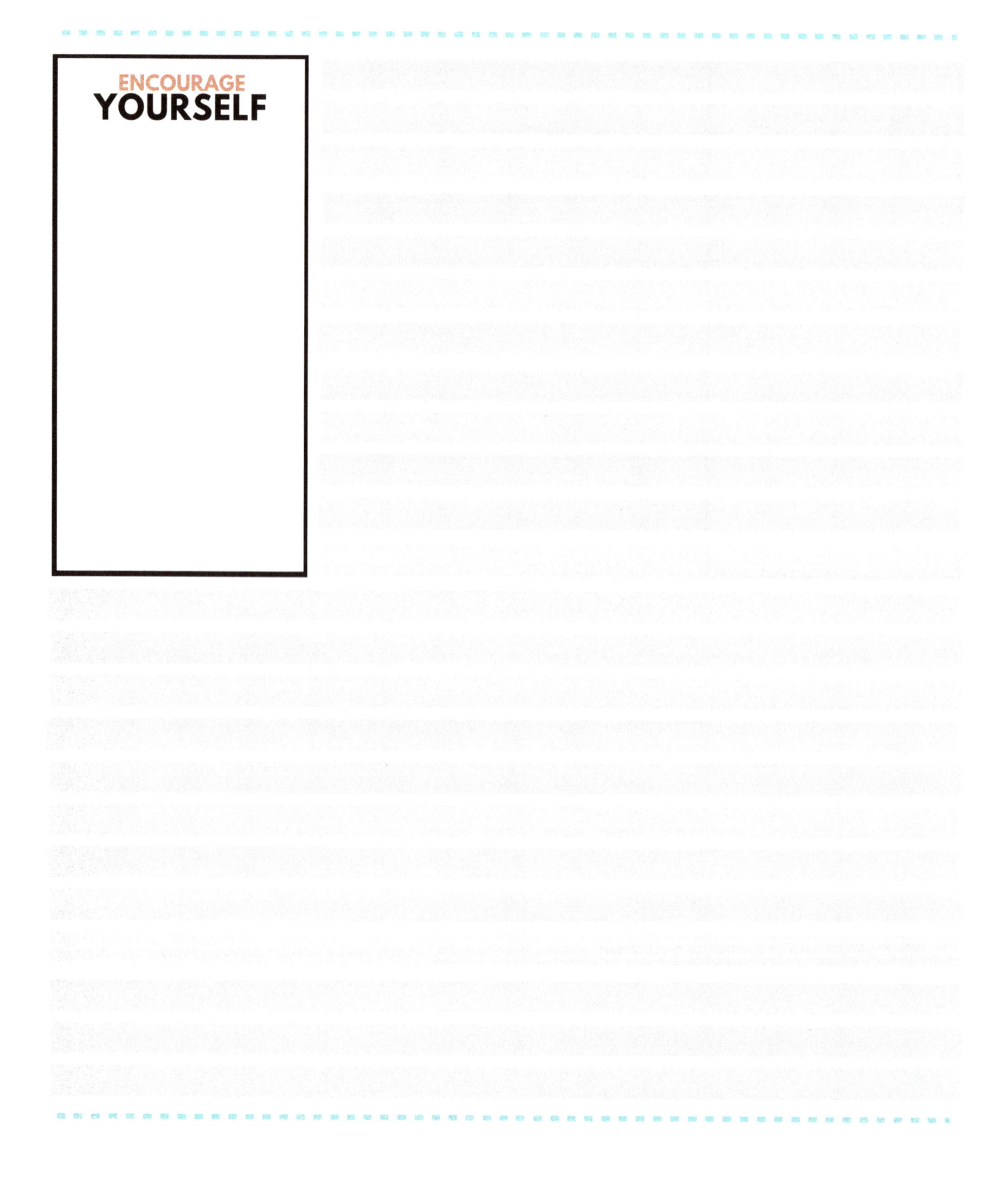

ENCOURAGE YOURSELF

END-OF-THE-DAY
RECAP & REVIEW

What are your thankful for today?

What battles did you win today?

What lessons did you learn today?

**AND WE KNOW THAT ALL THINGS WORK TOGETHER FOR GOOD TO THOSE WHO LOVE GOD, TO THOSE WHO ARE THE CALLED ACCORDING TO HIS PURPOSE.
ROMANS 8:28 (NKJV)**

What did God say to you today?

RECLAIM YOUR INHERITANCE

RECLAIM YOUR INHERITANCE

John 10:10 (AMP)
The thief comes only in order to steal and kill and destroy. I came that they may have and enjoy life, and have it in abundance [to the full, till it overflows].

John 10:7-8 (AMP)
So Jesus said again, "I assure you and most solemnly say to you, I am [a]the Door for the sheep [leading to life]. All who came before Me [as false messiahs and self-appointed leaders] are thieves and robbers, but the [true] sheep did not hear them.

YOU DON'T HAVE TO SETTLE FOR A JOYLESS OR COMPLACENT LIFE.

It's the middle of the night and a burglar slips in through your window while you were sleeping. In the dark of the night, he steals your TV, some of your kitchen appliances, and your car right from under you. Does this story sound realistic? It should because you've been letting the enemy steal from you for years. Instead of the TV, its been your faith. It wasn't the kitchen appliances but he got your joy. Oh look, there he goes again, running away with your peace. This is all your hard-earned, tribulation-tested sanctified stuff and the enemy has his little grimy hands all over it.

Are you mad? Did you even notice anything missing? I know you are probably saying that you wouldn't take an "L" like that but I can guarantee that you have. You lost your gratitude but did you see how you easily replaced it with complaining? The enemy took your peace and you replaced it with complacency when you told God you weren't going to move until He did something for you. The enemy stole your faith and you replaced it with doubt by saying I expected God to do > insert vanity here< and He didn't. Now you don't want to believe he will do anything because he didn't do that one thing. The enemy came in like a flood and you drowned.

Don't keep sinking; Rise above it by remembering who you belong to. Jesus's sacrifice on the cross means that you have access to enjoy life to the fullest. You don't have to settle for a joyless or complacent life. You also don't have to accept what life gives you. God gave you the ability, by grace, to live an abundant life but is up to you to reclaim it. If a bad situation greets you in the morning, you have a choice to give in to those bad thoughts that lead to complaining, unthankfulness, and doubt or you can choose not to hear it. You can hold that thought, feeling, and emotion captive (**2 Corinthians 10:5**) and replace it with what you were already promised. Reject what the enemy wants you to have and accept the peace, love, and abundance that is your heavenly and earthly inheritance.

RECLAIM YOUR INHERITANCE

What bad or negative thoughts do you allow to linger in your mind?

JESUS'S SACRIFICE ON THE CROSS MEANS THAT YOU HAVE ACCESS TO ENJOY LIFE TO THE FULLEST.

How do you plan to counteract negative thoughts, feelings, or emotions?

PRAYER
ACTION PLAN

SCRIPTURE: **DATE:**

PRAYER CHANGES EVERYTHING INCLUDING YOU

PRAYER LIST

- [ ]
- [ ]
- [ ]
- [ ]

PRAISE LIST

- [ ]
- [ ]
- [ ]
- [ ]

PRAYER AND REFLECTION

FAITH
ACTION PLAN

WHAT MOUNTAIN ARE WE MOVING TODAY?

RESOURCES

OBSTACLES

WHAT DOES IT PROFIT, MY BRETHREN, IF SOMEONE SAYS HE HAS FAITH BUT DOES NOT HAVE WORKS? JAMES 2:14 (NKJV)

TO-DAY LIST
- [ ]
- [ ]
- [ ]
- [ ]
- [ ]
- [ ]
- [ ]

ACTIONABLE STEPS
1.
2.
3.
4.
5.
6.
7.

THOUGHTS & IDEAS

JOURNAL YOUR HEART

Cast your burden on the Lord, And He shall sustain you;
He shall never permit the righteous to be moved.
Psalm 55:22 (NKJV)

CAST YOUR CARE

JOURNAL
YOUR FAITH

"Thus speaks the Lord God of Israel, saying: 'Write in a book for yourself all the words that I have spoken to you.
Jeremiah 30:2 (NKJV)

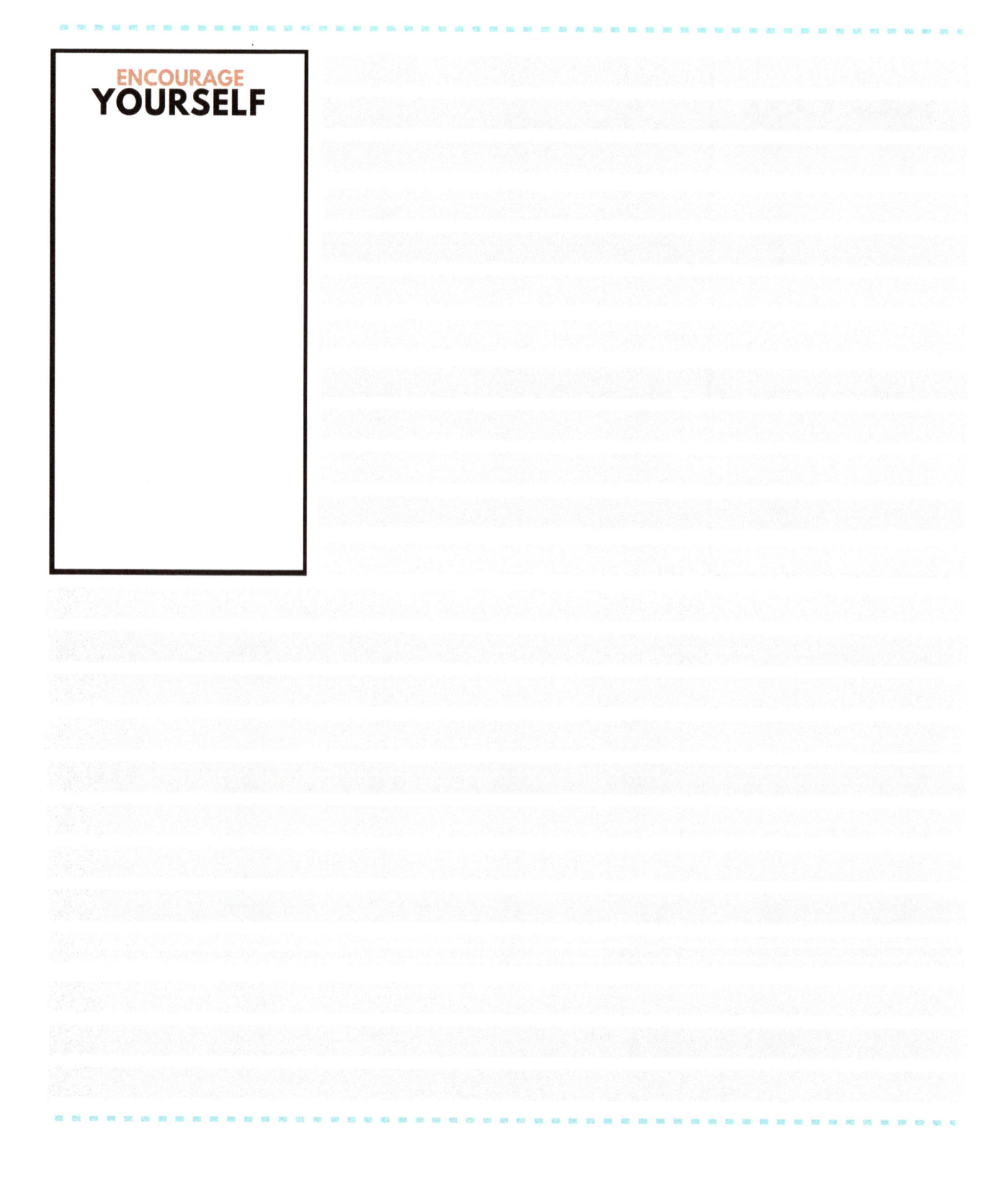

ENCOURAGE YOURSELF

END-OF-THE-DAY
RECAP & REVIEW

What are your thankful for today?

What battles did you win today?

What lessons did you learn today?

**AND WE KNOW THAT ALL THINGS WORK TOGETHER FOR GOOD TO THOSE WHO LOVE GOD, TO THOSE WHO ARE THE CALLED ACCORDING TO HIS PURPOSE.
ROMANS 8:28 (NKJV)**

What did God say to you today?

I AM FEARLESS
and confident because
GOD HELPS ME.

HE SUPPORTS ME
in all situations with His righteous
RIGHT HAND.

— ISAIAH 41:10 —

GUARD YOUR HEART

PROVERBS 4:23

GUARD YOUR HEART

Matthew 6:21 (AMP)
for where your treasure is, there your heart [your wishes, your desires; that on which your life centers] will be also.

Proverbs 3:5 (AMP)
Trust in and rely confidently on the Lord with all your heart And do not rely on your own insight or understanding.

YOUR HEART IS THE SEAT FOR YOUR RELATIONSHIP WITH GOD

I am an avid gamer. My mother gave me a PlayStation console when I was younger for Christmas and I have loved it ever since. One type of game that is popular is called first- person shooters or FPSs.(Don't revoke my Christian card.) This game has a high learning curve because you're typically tossed into a virtual world with no training or introduction. You have to learn the controls, gameplay, and strategies to try and overtake your opponent quickly. The other players don't care if you just started yesterday; They will ruthlessly take you out with no questions asked. No experience? Don't matter. No help? Don't matter. It's killed or be killed. I know this sounds kinda brutal but it honestly is because it's WAR.

Whether you want to acknowledge it or not you are in a war zone right now. The enemy knows this but we don't. I don't know why we, as the people of God, like playing hide and seek. We like to think that if we hide in Christ that the enemy won't seek us out. In **Job 1:7-10**, we see the enemy going to and fro looking for a way to destroy Job. He had already been there several times before God even brought Job up in conversation. What does that mean for you? It means the war had already started. He's already thrown his bombs and shot his arrows. You've felt the jabs and the punches just this year.

There have been so many trials, ways, and reasons why you should have lost your mind. PRAISE BREAK: BUT GOD. You survived. You survived the disappointment. You survived the heartbreak. Have you survived the loss? What if I told you that the enemy isn't after your family, friends, health, possessions, or mind? The enemy has plenty of money and plenty of people, even some of our own family and friends, that do his bidding. He's not after your status or even your praise. He is waging war over one thing and it's your heart.

Your heart is what makes a choice between loving God or hating him. Your heart is the seat for your relationship with God and the enemy's goal is to destroy every aspect of it. The enemy wants you to curse God because of what you have to endure with Him.(**Job 1:11**) Yes, in Christ you have to endure some horrible unfair circumstances but remember it's war. Bloodshed, sacrifice, and tears are factored in. Trouble will press you on every side.(**2 Corinthians 4:8**), but don't let your heart waver. Trust God at all times. He is good and loves you. When the war begins to wage upon you, stand firm, dismiss your understanding, and trust Him anyhow.

GUARD YOUR HEART

Describe your current relationship with God.

TROUBLE WILL PRESS YOU ON EVERY SIDE, BUT DON'T LET YOUR HEART WAVER.

Write a note to yourself that you can read when your relationship with God is being tested.

PRAYER
ACTION PLAN

SCRIPTURE: **DATE:**

PRAYER BRINGS PEACE TO A FRUSTRATED MIND

PRAYER LIST

- [ ]
- [ ]
- [ ]
- [ ]

PRAISE LIST

- [ ]
- [ ]
- [ ]
- [ ]

PRAYER AND REFLECTION

FAITH
ACTION PLAN

WHAT MOUNTAIN ARE WE MOVING TODAY?

RESOURCES

OBSTACLES

WHAT DOES IT PROFIT, MY BRETHREN, IF SOMEONE SAYS HE HAS FAITH BUT DOES NOT HAVE WORKS? JAMES 2:14 (NKJV)

TO-DAY LIST
- [ ]
- [ ]
- [ ]
- [ ]
- [ ]
- [ ]
- [ ]

ACTIONABLE STEPS
1.
2.
3.
4.
5.
6.
7.

THOUGHTS & IDEAS

JOURNAL YOUR HEART

Cast your burden on the Lord, And He shall sustain you;
He shall never permit the righteous to be moved.
Psalm 55:22 (NKJV)

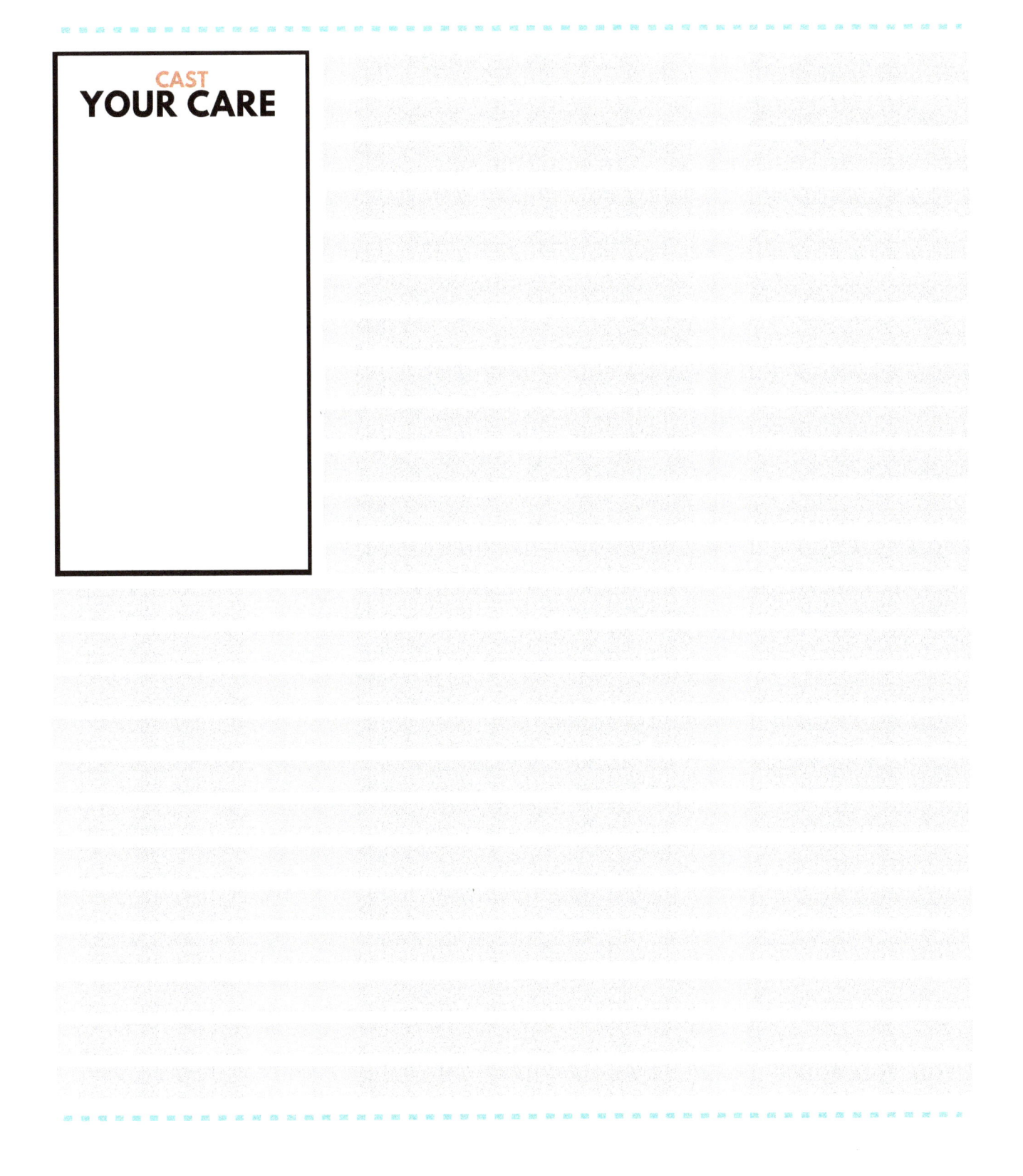

CAST YOUR CARE

JOURNAL YOUR FAITH

"Thus speaks the Lord God of Israel, saying: 'Write in a book for yourself all the words that I have spoken to you.
Jeremiah 30:2 (NKJV)

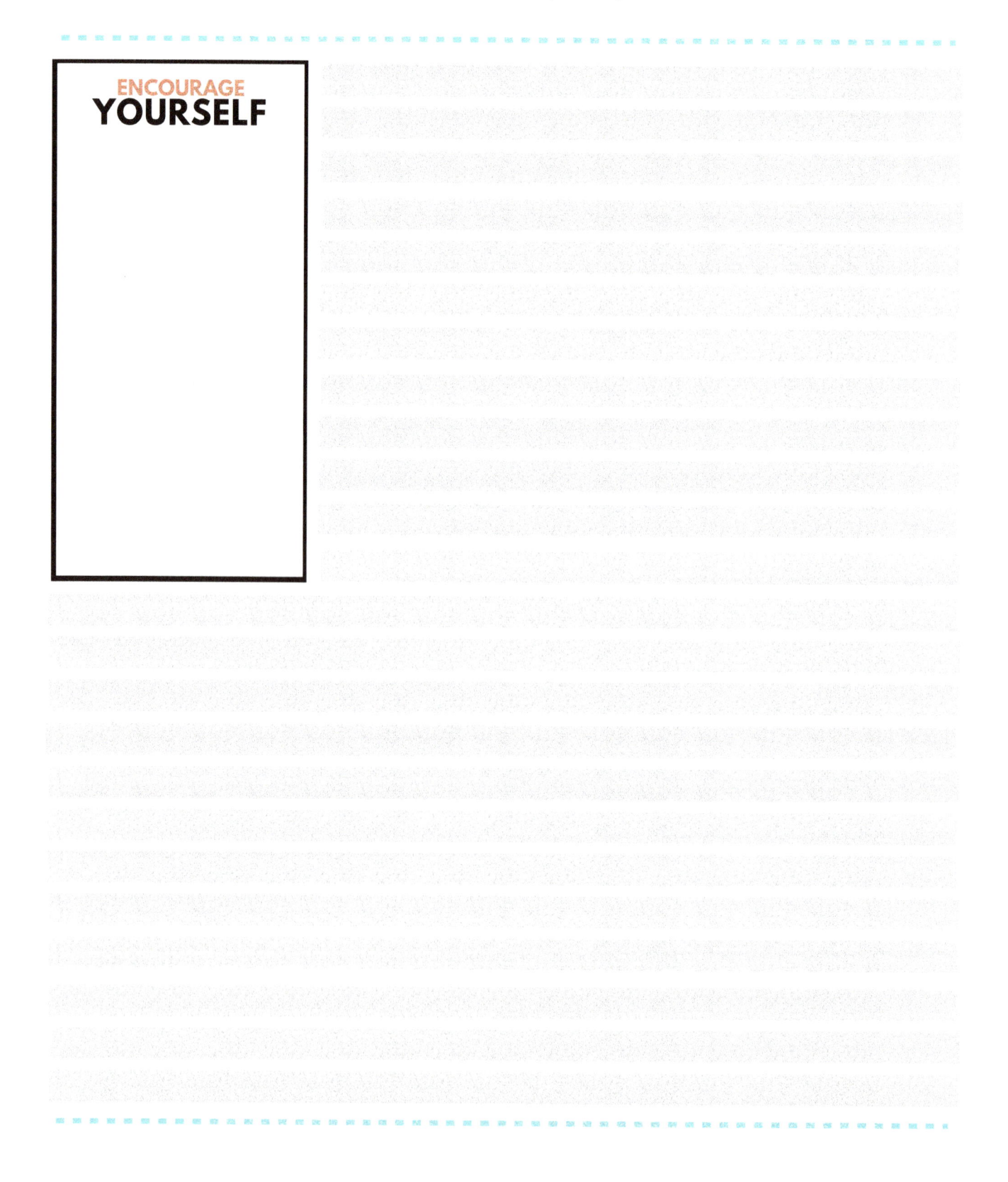

ENCOURAGE YOURSELF

END-OF-THE-DAY
RECAP & REVIEW

What are your thankful for today?

What battles did you win today?

What lessons did you learn today?

**AND WE KNOW THAT ALL THINGS WORK TOGETHER FOR GOOD TO THOSE WHO LOVE GOD, TO THOSE WHO ARE THE CALLED ACCORDING TO HIS PURPOSE.
ROMANS 8:28 (NKJV)**

What did God say to you today?

RULE YOUR SPIRIT

PROVERBS 16:32

RULE YOUR SPIRIT

2 Peter 1:5-9 (NKJV)
But also for this very reason, giving all diligence, add to your faith virtue, to virtue knowledge, to knowledge self-control, to self-control perseverance, to perseverance godliness, to godliness brotherly kindness, and to brotherly kindness love. For if these things are yours and abound, you will be neither barren nor unfruitful in the knowledge of our Lord Jesus Christ. For he who lacks these things is shortsighted, even to blindness, and has forgotten that he was cleansed from his old sins.

Proverbs 16:32 (NKJV)
He who is slow to anger is better than the mighty, And he who rules his spirit than he who takes a city.

WHAT ARE YOUR EMOTIONS COSTING YOU?

We are aware that God has a purposed plan for our lives. This is illustrated in **Jeremiah 29:11**. This plan, if we yield to the Holy Spirit can be a straight shot to God's will and destiny for our lives. There's only one problem: US. We will get in our own way in a heartbeat. God will say go left and we will insist on going right based on how we feel, not understanding that His ways are higher and there are far greater consequences.

There is a biblical example of a very large group, called the Israelites, who let their emotions get in the way of their promise. The Lord promised them a land flowing with milk and honey and He also told them that people were already in the land. They sent 12 people to spy out the land and they came back bearing witness to the promise with their own eyes but they felt like grasshoppers. It even goes on to say in **Numbers 14** that the Israelites wept all night, cried out in discontent, and ripped their clothes in grief. They were in a state of self-induced panic. They choose to follow their emotions and not believe God. Their brief emotional tantrum cost them 40 years. It's an eye-opening story but also a powerful lesson. Unruled emotions will ultimately lead you to forfeit your promise.

It was unruled emotion that almost prevented Naaman from getting his healing. (**2 Kings 5**) It was also unruled emotion that almost got Abigail's husband killed. (**1 Samuel 25**) What is your unruled emotion costing you? Furthermore, let's not forget that God has emotions too and they far outweigh yours. **The Lord said to Moses, "How long will these people treat me disrespectfully and reject Me? And how long will they not believe in Me, despite all the [miraculous] signs which I have performed among them? (Numbers 14:11).** You thought you were just complaining or venting but it was downright disrespectful to God. You thought being afraid was a reasonable excuse to abort God's plan but God took it as a sign of rejection. So, once again, what are your emotions costing you?

You cannot afford to let your emotions rule you. Practice self-control. **2 Peter 1 says to add self-control to knowledge.** It means that once you know better, do better! You are more than capable of ruling your anger, frustration, or sadness. You can't let your feelings have access to your faith. You can have emotions but they have to be properly submitted on the altar through prayer. (**1 Samuel 1**) So take back the reins. Reel it back in. Rule your spirit.

RULE YOUR
SPIRIT

Name some emotions that you often deal with and what causes them.

RULE YOUR SPIRIT

Write out a 5-Step plan for dealing with your emotions.

PRAYER
ACTION PLAN

SCRIPTURE: **DATE:**

PRAYER CHANGES EVERYTHING INCLUDING YOU

PRAYER LIST **PRAISE LIST**

- [ ]
- [ ]
- [ ]
- [ ]

- [ ]
- [ ]
- [ ]
- [ ]

PRAYER AND REFLECTION

FAITH
ACTION PLAN

WHAT MOUNTAIN ARE WE MOVING TODAY?

RESOURCES

OBSTACLES

WHAT DOES IT PROFIT, MY BRETHREN, IF SOMEONE SAYS HE HAS FAITH BUT DOES NOT HAVE WORKS? JAMES 2:14 (NKJV)

TO-DAY LIST

- [ ]
- [ ]
- [ ]
- [ ]
- [ ]
- [ ]
- [ ]

ACTIONABLE STEPS

1.
2.
3.
4.
5.
6.
7.

THOUGHTS & IDEAS

JOURNAL YOUR HEART

Cast your burden on the Lord, And He shall sustain you;
He shall never permit the righteous to be moved.
Psalm 55:22 (NKJV)

CAST YOUR CARE

JOURNAL YOUR FAITH

"Thus speaks the Lord God of Israel, saying: 'Write in a book for yourself all the words that I have spoken to you.
Jeremiah 30:2 (NKJV)

ENCOURAGE YOURSELF

END-OF-THE-DAY
RECAP & REVIEW

What are your thankful for today?

What battles did you win today?

What lessons did you learn today?

**AND WE KNOW THAT ALL THINGS WORK TOGETHER FOR GOOD TO THOSE WHO LOVE GOD, TO THOSE WHO ARE THE CALLED ACCORDING TO HIS PURPOSE.
ROMANS 8:28 (NKJV)**

What did God say to you today?

DON'T COME DOWN

NEHEMIAH 6:3

DON'T COME DOWN

Nehemiah 6:3 (NKJV)
So I sent messengers to them, saying, "I am doing a great work, so that I cannot come down. Why should the work cease while I leave it and go down to you?"

Colossians 3:2 (AMP)
Set your mind and keep focused habitually on the things above [the heavenly things], not on things that are on the earth [which have only temporal value].

DON'T GIVE UP. DON'T SLOW DOWN. DON'T COME DOWN.

It almost never fails that when we finally set out minds to accomplish what God told us to do that something or someone commands our attention. It asks for a seat at the table to discuss topics and agendas that aren't worth our time. Yet, we give in. We are fully aware that we have work to do but something in us tells us to go handle that problem. We come down and the work does not get completed. Stopping the work may have happened a lot in the past for you but today it's time to say "No, I cannot come down."

Saying no doesn't mean you are lying. It doesn't even mean that you are being rude or unpeaceful. No simply means you cannot allow the work to cease. It wasn't assigned to you by accident or choice. God gave it to you. It may look impossible, and it most assuredly is without God, but that is why you can't afford to take a break. It will take every effort, resolve, and due diligence to get your task done. You aren't just buying groceries. You are doing a GREAT work. Great works require focus and a prompt dismissal of distractions.

You may not be building a wall like Nehemiah but you are building something. This "something" is not here on earth yet but it needs to be. You are manifesting God's will in the earth. That little idea is the seed of big realities.**Your kingdom come. Your will be done, on earth as it is in heaven (Matthew 6:10 NKJV).** The vision God gave you is not about you nor is it for you. It is part of God's ultimate plan where heaven invades earth. It has a specific time and purpose and you can't allow anything to make you lose focus. It is your heavenly mandate to finish the work.

Nehemiah was appointed to build the wall and he did. The wall was magnificent and he had only one thing left which was to hang the doors. His enemies heard that he was building a wall and they sent messengers to Nehemiah asking for him to meet with them and discuss rumors. Good thing Nehemiah knew better. His response was this: **Then I sent to him, saying, "No such things as you say are being done, but you invent them in your own heart." For they all were trying to make us afraid, saying, "Their hands will be weakened in the work, and it will not be done." Now therefore, O God, strengthen my hands.**

The enemy has sent messengers disguised as distractions for 3 reasons: To make you afraid, weaken your hands and stop the work. You might be afraid of how big the vision is that God gave you. You might even be afraid of the unwanted attention from people. They might ask you why you feel qualified to do the work. Just like Nehemiah ignore it. God appointed you and that's all the approval you need. Those distractions are also sent with the intention to weaken your hands or cause you to doubt. Don't allow them to. It may be a monumental endeavor and you probably won't be able to see anything coming together but that does not mean the work must stop. It may seem impossible but do it anyway. Don't come down. It will work out in the end. Keep pressing. Don't give up. Don't slow down. Don't come down.

DON'T COME DOWN

Nehemiah was appointed to build a wall. What is God appointing you to do?

THAT LITTLE IDEA IS THE SEED OF BIG REALITIES.

It's time to be preemptive. Write out 3 ways you can politely say "No". Program these polite no's as a response in your email and text messages and use them whenever necessary.

PRAYER
ACTION PLAN

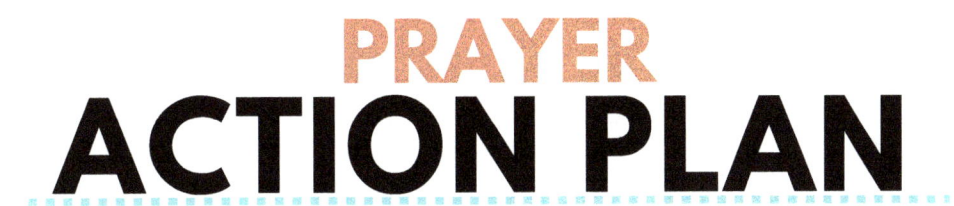

SCRIPTURE: **DATE:**

PRAYER EMPOWERS YOU

PRAYER LIST

- [ ]
- [ ]
- [ ]
- [ ]

PRAISE LIST

- [ ]
- [ ]
- [ ]
- [ ]

PRAYER AND REFLECTION

FAITH ACTION PLAN

WHAT MOUNTAIN ARE WE MOVING TODAY?

RESOURCES

OBSTACLES

WHAT DOES IT PROFIT, MY BRETHREN, IF SOMEONE SAYS HE HAS FAITH BUT DOES NOT HAVE WORKS? JAMES 2:14 (NKJV)

TO-DAY LIST

- [ ]
- [ ]
- [ ]
- [ ]
- [ ]
- [ ]
- [ ]

ACTIONABLE STEPS

1.
2.
3.
4.
5.
6.
7.

THOUGHTS & IDEAS

JOURNAL YOUR HEART

Cast your burden on the Lord, And He shall sustain you;
He shall never permit the righteous to be moved.
Psalm 55:22 (NKJV)

CAST YOUR CARE

JOURNAL YOUR FAITH

"Thus speaks the Lord God of Israel, saying: 'Write in a book for yourself all the words that I have spoken to you.
Jeremiah 30:2 (NKJV)

ENCOURAGE YOURSELF

END-OF-THE-DAY
RECAP & REVIEW

What are your thankful for today?

What battles did you win today?

What lessons did you learn today?

AND WE KNOW THAT ALL THINGS WORK TOGETHER FOR GOOD TO THOSE WHO LOVE GOD, TO THOSE WHO ARE THE CALLED ACCORDING TO HIS PURPOSE.
ROMANS 8:28 (NKJV)

What did God say to you today?

FEAR IS FAKE

PSALM 56:3-4

FEAR IS FAKE

Isaiah 41:10 (NKJV)
Fear not, for I am with you;
Be not dismayed, for I am your God.
I will strengthen you,
Yes, I will help you,
I will uphold you with My righteous right hand.

2 Timothy 1:7 (NKJV)
For God has not given us a spirit of fear, but of power and of love and of a sound mind.

THEY KEY TO IT ALL IS TO REMAIN SURRENDERED

I hear a lot of people talk about fear and how to essentially conquer it. They always mention rising over it or courage but I rarely hear about surrender. A surrendered soul has no choice but to be strong and courageous. Many biblical characters are honored as being fearless in the sight of opposition. People like Jesus, Stephen, Paul, Gideon, David, and Joshua have that reputation but a little examination would show us that a fearless mind comes from a heart of surrender.

Take Joshua for example. God told him to go and possess the land that Joshua got a glimpse of nearly 40 years prior. He told him what we love to put on a t-shirt. " **Be strong and very courageous**" (**Joshua 1:7**) But do you think this could have happened without a heart that was surrendered to God? Joshua was old. He was well past his prime and probably the last person you would choose on your dodgeball team yet he went. I am sure he was like" really God? Now?" He had experienced quite a hardship traveling around in circles. I'm sure he wasn't pleased to outright go to war but he surrendered. He said " you got it, God. Now, what do you want me to do?" This is the mindset that makes fear diminish.

To paint the picture honestly, fear never takes a backseat. It will always find a way to scream loudly at your vision and when one fear is defeated... another one will rise up. They key to it all is to remain surrendered, not to the fear but to God. A surrendered heart puts all the eggs in one basket. It says yes even when life goes crazy and everything stops making sense. A surrendered soul will accept help however the Lord provides it. It doesn't revel in the situation, even if life is at stake. It moves according to the Will of God. That fear, that very thing that you are afraid of is really afraid of you. God did not give you a spirit of fear but that doesn't mean your opposition doesn't have it. Trust me, they are very afraid of God and you (**Joshua 5:1**). You are a threat to their existence and they know it.

Remember that fear is fake. God walks with you and He will give you all the strength necessary to overcome whatever adversary you face. You don't have to remain the victim when you walk in victory. There is enough power and love within you and with you to completely obliterate anything standing in your way. So...use it.

FEAR IS FAKE

What are you afraid of?

YOU DON'T HAVE TO REMAIN THE VICTIM WHEN YOU WALK IN VICTORY.

What does the word "Fearless" mean to you?

PRAYER
ACTION PLAN

SCRIPTURE: **DATE:**

PRAYER CHANGES EVERYTHING INCLUDING YOU

PRAYER LIST

- [ ]
- [ ]
- [ ]
- [ ]

PRAISE LIST

- [ ]
- [ ]
- [ ]
- [ ]

PRAYER AND REFLECTION

FAITH
ACTION PLAN

WHAT MOUNTAIN ARE WE MOVING TODAY?

RESOURCES

OBSTACLES

WHAT DOES IT PROFIT, MY BRETHREN, IF SOMEONE SAYS HE HAS FAITH BUT DOES NOT HAVE WORKS? JAMES 2:14 (NKJV)

TO-DAY LIST

- [ ]
- [ ]
- [ ]
- [ ]
- [ ]
- [ ]
- [ ]

ACTIONABLE STEPS

1.
2.
3.
4.
5.
6.
7.

THOUGHTS & IDEAS

JOURNAL YOUR HEART

Cast your burden on the Lord, And He shall sustain you;
He shall never permit the righteous to be moved.
Psalm 55:22 (NKJV)

CAST YOUR CARE

JOURNAL YOUR FAITH

"Thus speaks the Lord God of Israel, saying: 'Write in a book for yourself all the words that I have spoken to you.
Jeremiah 30:2 (NKJV)

ENCOURAGE YOURSELF

END-OF-THE-DAY
RECAP & REVIEW

What are your thankful for today?

What battles did you win today?

What lessons did you learn today?

**AND WE KNOW THAT ALL THINGS WORK TOGETHER FOR GOOD TO THOSE WHO LOVE GOD, TO THOSE WHO ARE THE CALLED ACCORDING TO HIS PURPOSE.
ROMANS 8:28 (NKJV)**

What did God say to you today?

I AM POWERFUL LOVING AND SELF-DISCIPLINED

2 TIMOTHY 1:7

HE GIVES AND HE TAKES

JOB 1:21

HE GIVES
AND HE TAKES

Job 1:21 (AMP)
He said, "Naked (without possessions) I came [into this world] from my mother's womb, And naked I will return there. The Lord gave and the Lord has taken away; Blessed be the name of the Lord."

Philippians 4:12-13 (NKJV)
I know how to be abased, and I know how to abound. Everywhere and in all things I have learned both to be full and to be hungry, both to abound and to suffer need. I can do all things through Christ who strengthens me.

FOR EVERY LOSS, THERE WILL BE A GAIN.

I remember the day I got saved. It was at a college bible study. I'm not even sure why I went but something inside me told me that I should go. It was one of the greatest experiences of my life. I had never experienced such freedom and peace in my life before that. God revealed himself to me on thursday night and, unbeknownst me, it would be the start of a very difficult journey.

My story is not like most stories. When you hear about how people got saved it's usually after they were close to death or at the worst point in their life. Then salvation comes. They intersect with God and everything changes. The clouds go away, the sun shines, and what's left is an amazing happily ever after. The " happily ever after" didn't happen for me. I was on my way up when Jesus showed up. I was in an early entrance program for college and I recently received an acceptance letter to my dream school. I felt unstoppable. Yet something inside me told me to ask God about it. I warred within myself. Part of me felt like God would want this for me and the other felt like it would be an entirely wrong decision. I decided to pray anyway and my heart sank when I found the answer. He said no. It took years for me to recover from that one "no". Many more circumstances some good and some terribly tragic followed that beautiful moment in bible study.

I know that it can be very difficult to understand why the Lord takes. In fact, we as followers of Christ, have to accept the peace that surpasses the ability to understand.(**Philippians 4:7**) Tragedy befalls us. Poverty knocks on our door. We are pressed on every side.(**2 Corinthians 4:8**) The pain can be crippling but there is a solemn fact about losing people, things, and hope that we can be assured of: It will change. If you're reading this in a very dark moment in your life please know that circumstances do change. Today might not be a good day and that's okay because tomorrow may be better. Next week may be better, and next year may be better. God never changes but seasons do. He takes but He also gives. For every loss, there will be a gain, just as sure as winter turns into spring. Even the worst circumstances will turn out for your good.(**Romans 8:28**) Appreciate the highs and lows of every season and brave it out wholeheartedly. Live out whatever lot you have. Don't give in to dark thoughts. I tear down thoughts of suicide/homicide even as you read these words. You can endure this hardship because you can do all things through Christ (**Philippians 4:13**). Accept His strength. God still has a plan for you and just as the sunsets, it will also rise. Rise with it.

HE GIVES
AND HE TAKES

What are some things that God has taken from you?

LIVE OUT WHATEVER LOT YOU HAVE.

What are some things God has given you?

PRAYER
ACTION PLAN

SCRIPTURE: **DATE:**

PRAYER STRENGTHENS YOU

PRAYER LIST

- [ ]
- [ ]
- [ ]
- [ ]

PRAISE LIST

- [ ]
- [ ]
- [ ]
- [ ]

PRAYER AND REFLECTION

FAITH
ACTION PLAN

WHAT MOUNTAIN ARE WE MOVING TODAY?

RESOURCES

OBSTACLES

WHAT DOES IT PROFIT, MY BRETHREN, IF SOMEONE SAYS HE HAS FAITH BUT DOES NOT HAVE WORKS? JAMES 2:14 (NKJV)

TO-DAY LIST

- [ ]
- [ ]
- [ ]
- [ ]
- [ ]
- [ ]
- [ ]

ACTIONABLE STEPS

1.
2.
3.
4.
5.
6.
7.

THOUGHTS & IDEAS

JOURNAL
YOUR HEART

Cast your burden on the Lord, And He shall sustain you;
He shall never permit the righteous to be moved.
Psalm 55:22 (NKJV)

CAST
YOUR CARE

JOURNAL YOUR FAITH

"Thus speaks the Lord God of Israel, saying: 'Write in a book for yourself all the words that I have spoken to you.
Jeremiah 30:2 (NKJV)

ENCOURAGE YOURSELF

END-OF-THE-DAY
RECAP & REVIEW

What are your thankful for today?

What battles did you win today?

What lessons did you learn today?

AND WE KNOW THAT ALL THINGS WORK TOGETHER FOR GOOD TO THOSE WHO LOVE GOD, TO THOSE WHO ARE THE CALLED ACCORDING TO HIS PURPOSE.
ROMANS 8:28 (NKJV)

What did God say to you today?

YOU'RE GRACED FOR THIS

2 CORINTHIANS 12:9

YOU'RE GRACED FOR THIS

2 Corinthians 12:8-9 (NKJV)
Concerning this thing I pleaded with the Lord three times that it might depart from me. And He said to me, "My grace is sufficient for you, for My strength is made perfect in weakness." Therefore most gladly I will rather boast in my infirmities, that the power of Christ may rest upon me.

Romans 6:1(AMP)
Believers Are Dead to Sin, Alive to God
What shall we say [to all this]? Should we continue in sin and practice sin as a habit so that [God's gift of] grace may increase and overflow?

GRACE WILL COVER US UNTIL IT DOESN'T

Grace is strength and favor and I'm going to skip straight to point on this one and tell you to stop using it for your own purpose and plans. It was grace that Jonah used when he chose to disobey God (**Jonah 1**). Grace was used by Moses when he struck the rock (**Numbers 20**). Grace used by David when he destroyed Uriah and slept with Bathsheba (**2 Samuel 11**). Grace is powerful because it covers us from the mighty hand of God that should have smacked the taste out of our mouths for being disobedient. Sometimes I wish our parents had that grace lol. But seriously what are you using your grace for? Good or Evil? God's unmerited favor should promote movement IN God's will not out of it.

I understand it, though. There are many times in our lives that we feel like God has put too much on our shoulders. We plead, just like Paul for it to to be taken away but God's grace is sufficient. This means that you have enough strength to triumph. This doesn't mean that you are strong. In fact, it means that you are very weak. This weakness implies that what you are facing produces deficiencies within you. The power you lack should show you where you end and it should also remind you that it is at that point that God's strength begins. He is not expecting for you to be able to withstand it all. He is expecting for you to be vulnerable enough to accept His strength and not perish in your own.

You're not perfect and you should boldly admit it. You may sin knowingly and unknowingly. There may still be some pitfalls that you are struggling to overcome and it's okay. The issue happens if you continue it and practice sin. There might be a struggle but there should also be a stopping point. God provides a way out of every temptation and you should be fighting to find it(**1 Corinthians 10:13**). There is sufficient repentance but there is no sufficient excuse. We can't continually practice things we know that we should not be doing. Doing that is a sin (**James 4:17**). Sin is not offensive to God because of what it does to Him. It offensive to God because of what it does to us. Sinful acts lead to death. It kills you sometimes bit by bit or immediately. You wouldn't want that for your children so why should God? The flesh craves the grave (**Romans 8:6**). It wants to find the fastest route out of here which is why we can't continue to abound in fleshly decisions. Grace will cover us until it doesn't. Don't end up in the belly of a whale. Do what God tells you to do. You're graced for this.

YOU'RE GRACED FOR THIS

Describe a moment or time when you practiced sin. What were the consequences?

GOD'S UNMERITED FAVOR SHOULD PROMOTE MOVEMENT IN GOD'S WILL NOT OUT OF IT.

What does grace mean to you? Describe a time when grace covered you.

PRAYER
ACTION PLAN

SCRIPTURE: **DATE:**

PRAYER CHANGES EVERYTHING INCLUDING YOU

PRAYER LIST

- [ ]
- [ ]
- [ ]
- [ ]

PRAISE LIST

- [ ]
- [ ]
- [ ]
- [ ]

PRAYER AND REFLECTION

FAITH
ACTION PLAN

WHAT MOUNTAIN ARE WE MOVING TODAY?

RESOURCES

OBSTACLES

WHAT DOES IT PROFIT, MY BRETHREN, IF SOMEONE SAYS HE HAS FAITH BUT DOES NOT HAVE WORKS? JAMES 2:14 (NKJV)

TO-DAY LIST

- [ ]
- [ ]
- [ ]
- [ ]
- [ ]
- [ ]
- [ ]

ACTIONABLE STEPS

1.
2.
3.
4.
5.
6.
7.

THOUGHTS & IDEAS

JOURNAL YOUR HEART

Cast your burden on the Lord, And He shall sustain you;
He shall never permit the righteous to be moved.
Psalm 55:22 (NKJV)

CAST YOUR CARE

JOURNAL YOUR FAITH

"Thus speaks the Lord God of Israel, saying: 'Write in a book for yourself all the words that I have spoken to you.
Jeremiah 30:2 (NKJV)

ENCOURAGE YOURSELF

END-OF-THE-DAY
RECAP & REVIEW

What are your thankful for today?

What battles did you win today?

What lessons did you learn today?

**AND WE KNOW THAT ALL THINGS WORK TOGETHER FOR GOOD TO THOSE WHO LOVE GOD, TO THOSE WHO ARE THE CALLED ACCORDING TO HIS PURPOSE.
ROMANS 8:28 (NKJV)**

What did God say to you today?

I WILL NOT COMPLAIN

— PHILIPPIANS 2:14 —

DON'T WORRY ABOUT IT

MATTHEW 6:25

DON'T WORRY ABOUT IT

Matthew 6:31-33 (NKJV)
"Therefore do not worry, saying, 'What shall we eat?' or 'What shall we drink?' or 'What shall we wear?' For after all these things the Gentiles seek. For your heavenly Father knows that you need all these things. But seek first the kingdom of God and His righteousness, and all these things shall be added to you.

Philippians 4:6 (NKJV)
Be anxious for nothing, but in everything by prayer and supplication, with thanksgiving, let your requests be made known to God;

GOD KNOWS WHAT YOU NEED.

We've all been there. Our friends want to go out to dinner but we check our bank account and the balance reads $1.62. The rent is due and you're already a day late and a dollar short. The bills are screaming at you and you're left facing the uncomfortable decision of whether to pay tithes or your light bill. However you split it, there is just not enough money to go around. You've taken all job opportunities and worked all the shifts available. You pray relentlessly for an increase. Does this sound familiar? Money is such a difficult issue for us Christians. We believe in a God that can do the impossible but are faced with the constant reality of being financially unstable and in constant lack. Is this what God wants for us? Why won't God move? These are valid questions. We're going to explore the truth about money in God's word and discuss ways to finally beat financial anxiety. (Yes it can be done.)

The word discusses financial worry or anxiety in detail in Matthew 6. Before we continue we must establish one foundational truth. God's word is the complete truth. I know this may sound a bit elementary but many don't read the word much less believe it. In order the get free from anxiety, we must come to terms with the fact that the word of God (the Bible) is absolute truth. It is just as Jesus spoke in Matthew 4:10. When the devil came to tempt him, Jesus refuted him with " it is written". Our journey from anxiety to peace is rooted in God's word. Through our circumstances, emotions, and harsh realities we have to still stand on God's word and the undeniable notion that God's word will NOT fail. Can you believe that? If not then stop reading now and take a moment to pray on this subject. Ask God to help your unbelief and to renew your faith. This process is not a simple one but deliverance from financial worry can be achieved if we are honest with where we stand.

As stated before, Matthew 6 is a key scripture for defeating all worry including financially related ones. God knows what you need. I will repeat it again. God knows what you need. He is fully aware that you have bills and obligations. He can see what your income is because He gave it to you. The Lord makes sure that His birds don't starve. Look outside on an early morning and see. How much more will He take care of you? This is why you can't just read the word of God. You have to believe it. God will not let you waste away. His word guarantees it.Pray about it but don't worry about it. Don't spend another minute being anxious or worried about your future. Just be thankful for today and the abounding provision that lies within it.

DON'T WORRY ABOUT IT

What are some circumstances that cause you to worry?

PRAY ABOUT IT BUT DON'T WORRY ABOUT IT.

Explain how God provides for you.

PRAYER
ACTION PLAN

SCRIPTURE: **DATE:**

PRAYER STRENGTHENS YOU

PRAYER LIST   **PRAISE LIST**

- [ ]
- [ ]
- [ ]
- [ ]

PRAYER AND REFLECTION

FAITH
ACTION PLAN

WHAT MOUNTAIN ARE WE MOVING TODAY?

RESOURCES

OBSTACLES

WHAT DOES IT PROFIT, MY BRETHREN, IF SOMEONE SAYS HE HAS FAITH BUT DOES NOT HAVE WORKS? JAMES 2:14 (NKJV)

TO-DAY LIST

- [ ]
- [ ]
- [ ]
- [ ]
- [ ]
- [ ]
- [ ]

ACTIONABLE STEPS

1.
2.
3.
4.
5.
6.
7.

THOUGHTS & IDEAS

JOURNAL YOUR HEART

Cast your burden on the Lord, And He shall sustain you;
He shall never permit the righteous to be moved.
Psalm 55:22 (NKJV)

CAST YOUR CARE

JOURNAL YOUR FAITH

"Thus speaks the Lord God of Israel, saying: 'Write in a book for yourself all the words that I have spoken to you.
Jeremiah 30:2 (NKJV)

ENCOURAGE YOURSELF

END-OF-THE-DAY
RECAP & REVIEW

What are your thankful for today?

What battles did you win today?

What lessons did you learn today?

**AND WE KNOW THAT ALL THINGS WORK TOGETHER FOR GOOD TO THOSE WHO LOVE GOD, TO THOSE WHO ARE THE CALLED ACCORDING TO HIS PURPOSE.
ROMANS 8:28 (NKJV)**

What did God say to you today?

DON'T DESPISE SMALL BEGINNINGS

ZECHARIAH 4:10

DON'T DESPISE
SMALL BEGINNINGS

Zechariah 4:10 (AMP)
Who [with reason] despises the day of small things (beginnings)? For these [a]seven [eyes] shall rejoice when they see the plumb line in the hand of Zerubbabel. They are the eyes of the Lord which roam throughout the earth."

1 Kings 18:44 (AMP)
And at the seventh time the servant said, "A cloud as small as a man's hand is coming up from the sea." And Elijah said, "Go up, say to Ahab, 'Prepare your chariot and go down, so that the rain shower does not stop you.'"

BE FAITHFUL WITH WHAT YOU HAVE.

So i'm sitting here playing a game that was my favorite pastime as a child. If you don't know already, the whole premise of the game is to travel around in a virtual world and catch animals. I've been working hard to get to a certain level in the game. One major factor to becoming great in the game is to catch rare and/or powerful animals. It's very similar to fishing. I sat in one area with all my gear and used advanced items to attract something rare but I couldn't seem to catch anything good. Everything I caught was either weak or common. Fortunately, you are able to gain experience with any capture. I really didn't want any more small catches. I already had hundreds of them. Yet and still everything that came my way was small. Then God showed me something. Yes, I believe that God can bring revelation from anything just as He created all we see from nothing. #movingon

I kept getting upset from attracting the weak catches. They were a dime a dozen but God showed me something. Each catch was an opportunity to gain experience no matter how big or small. I wonder how many opportunities I missed because I deemed them too small? The word says **Luke 16:10(AMP)** that **He who is faithful in a very little thing is also faithful in much; and he who is dishonest in a very little thing is also dishonest in much**. We have to remember that doing our very best in the small endeavors will ensure our victory in the larger ones. Every little thing is an opportunity to gain something that God knows we need. Every opportunity is a chance to grow. Don't get angry because you're tired of the little stuff like my fish analogy. Be faithful with what you have. Exhaust it. Multiply it just as the faithful servants in the parable of the talents(**Matthew 25**).

Don't complain either. Complaining will not add to your life. Come to God with thanksgiving and your request then wait(**Philippians 4:6**). Wait on it like Elijah waited on the rain. It may look small now but you have to prepare for the increase. You have to prepare for the day when you make that big catch or land that awesome opportunity.

Each little thing will eventually add up to something larger than our eyes can see. One raindrop is not very threatening but millions could cause a catastrophe. #askNoah Don't despise the small beginnings. Your gains may be in small increments now but if you're faithful, God will increase your labor into a fruitful harvest.

DON'T DESPISE
SMALL BEGINNINGS

Everything starts small. What are some small things in your life that can grow to become big things?

ONE RAINDROP IS NOT VERY THREATENING BUT MILLIONS COULD CAUSE A CATASTROPHE.

Big things can happen! Describe one opportunity that you want God to orchestrate.

PRAYER
ACTION PLAN

SCRIPTURE: **DATE:**

PRAYER CHANGES EVERYTHING INCLUDING YOU

PRAYER LIST

- [ ]
- [ ]
- [ ]
- [ ]

PRAISE LIST

- [ ]
- [ ]
- [ ]
- [ ]

PRAYER AND REFLECTION

FAITH
ACTION PLAN

WHAT MOUNTAIN ARE WE MOVING TODAY?

RESOURCES

OBSTACLES

WHAT DOES IT PROFIT, MY BRETHREN, IF SOMEONE SAYS HE HAS FAITH BUT DOES NOT HAVE WORKS? JAMES 2:14 (NKJV)

TO-DAY LIST

- [ ]
- [ ]
- [ ]
- [ ]
- [ ]
- [ ]
- [ ]

ACTIONABLE STEPS

1.
2.
3.
4.
5.
6.
7.

THOUGHTS & IDEAS

JOURNAL YOUR HEART

Cast your burden on the Lord, And He shall sustain you;
He shall never permit the righteous to be moved.
Psalm 55:22 (NKJV)

CAST YOUR CARE

JOURNAL YOUR FAITH

"Thus speaks the Lord God of Israel, saying: 'Write in a book for yourself all the words that I have spoken to you.
Jeremiah 30:2 (NKJV)

ENCOURAGE YOURSELF

END-OF-THE-DAY
RECAP & REVIEW

What are your thankful for today?

What battles did you win today?

What lessons did you learn today?

**AND WE KNOW THAT ALL THINGS WORK TOGETHER FOR GOOD TO THOSE WHO LOVE GOD, TO THOSE WHO ARE THE CALLED ACCORDING TO HIS PURPOSE.
ROMANS 8:28 (NKJV)**

What did God say to you today?

GIANTS DO FALL

1 SAMUEL 17

GIANTS DO FALL

1 Samuel 17:49-50 (AMP)
David put his hand into his bag and took out a stone and slung it, and it struck the Philistine on his forehead. The stone penetrated his forehead, and he fell face down on the ground. So David triumphed over the Philistine with a sling and a stone, and he struck down the Philistine and killed him; but there was no sword in David's hand.

Romans 8:37 (AMP)
Yet in all these things we are more than conquerors and gain an overwhelming victory through Him who loved us [so much that He died for us].

THOSE GIANTS CAN'T STOP YOU.

At some point, you are going to face a giant. Giants don't look menacing, but they are. What you'll find out is that a giant is something that you cannot fight on your own. They look dangerous and they are dangerous. They look larger than life and they are larger than life. A giant is something that stands in your way. They have space they're taking up but they also have everything else to back them up as well. The thing is we have to remember one thing when we face the giant and it's the same thing that David remembered. We don't have to fight them. Yes, we have to bring the rocks and yes we have to bring the slingshot. We also have to have the courage to use them. But the battle is not ours and the fight is not ours.

God fights for us.(**Exodus 14:14**) It may not seem that way. Actually, it always seems like our enemies are always winning. It looks like there's more than enough to go around for them. It seems like we have to beg for all the scraps. But their "winning" won't last forever. So just like Goliath, the enemy gets to taunt you for a while and the enemy gets to flaunt his strength. You might be afraid. You might get fearful but when the time comes Goliath will fall. You will become the victor. It won't be by your strength or by your might. It will be by the strength and power of God.(**Zechariah 4:6**) So take your slingshot, take your stance and fire away. Use whatever you have. Those giants can't stop you. Poverty can't stop you. People can't stop you. Don't faint. Don't quit and don't give up. Keep pressing forward. Come hell or high water keep pressing forward.

You are more than a conquer. You were not made to simply endure life. You were made to conquer it. The purpose on your life is so big that you have to continue until the end. Don't back down until you've seen it all. **Psalm 27:13** says that **I would have despaired had I not believed that I would see the goodness of the Lord in the land of the living(AMP)**. The very same David that defeated a lion, a bear and Goliath wrote this passage. This means that conquerers will lose heart if they don't believe. Don't fall into despair. Encourage yourself. Believe that there is a future victory beyond the day to day battles. If anything stands in your way today, grab what you have, put on your shield of faith(**Ephesians 6:16**) and stand firm. That giant will fall.

GIANTS DO FALL

What giants are you facing?

YOU WERE NOT MADE TO SIMPLY ENDURE LIFE. YOU WERE MADE TO CONQUER IT.

David used a slingshot and rock to defeat his giant. What can you use to defeat yours?

PRAYER
ACTION PLAN

SCRIPTURE: **DATE:**

PRAYER STRENGTHENS YOU

PRAYER LIST

- [ ]
- [ ]
- [ ]
- [ ]

PRAISE LIST

- [ ]
- [ ]
- [ ]
- [ ]

PRAYER AND REFLECTION

FAITH
ACTION PLAN

WHAT MOUNTAIN ARE WE MOVING TODAY?

RESOURCES

OBSTACLES

WHAT DOES IT PROFIT, MY BRETHREN, IF SOMEONE SAYS HE HAS FAITH BUT DOES NOT HAVE WORKS? JAMES 2:14 (NKJV)

TO-DAY LIST

- [ ]
- [ ]
- [ ]
- [ ]
- [ ]
- [ ]
- [ ]

ACTIONABLE STEPS

1.
2.
3.
4.
5.
6.
7.

THOUGHTS & IDEAS

JOURNAL YOUR HEART

Cast your burden on the Lord, And He shall sustain you;
He shall never permit the righteous to be moved.
Psalm 55:22 (NKJV)

CAST YOUR CARE

JOURNAL YOUR FAITH

"Thus speaks the Lord God of Israel, saying: 'Write in a book for yourself all the words that I have spoken to you.
Jeremiah 30:2 (NKJV)

ENCOURAGE YOURSELF

END-OF-THE-DAY
RECAP & REVIEW

What are your thankful for today?

What battles did you win today?

What lessons did you learn today?

AND WE KNOW THAT ALL THINGS WORK TOGETHER FOR GOOD TO THOSE WHO LOVE GOD, TO THOSE WHO ARE THE CALLED ACCORDING TO HIS PURPOSE.
ROMANS 8:28 (NKJV)

What did God say to you today?

PRESS

EQUALS

PROGRESS

PHILIPPIANS 3:14

PRESS EQUALS PROGRESS

Philippians 3:13-14 (AMP)
Brothers and sisters, I do not consider that I have made it my own yet; but one thing I do: forgetting what lies behind and reaching forward to what lies ahead, I press on toward the goal to win the [heavenly] prize of the upward call of God in Christ Jesus.

Philippians 1:6 (AMP)
I am convinced and confident of this very thing, that He who has begun a good work in you will [continue to] perfect and complete it until the day of Christ Jesus [the time of His return].

THE PRESS IS NOT IN VAIN.

History has a way of repeating itself. You can see it when the latest fashion trends look like the same clothes from two decades ago. We as humans, also do repetitive things. We get up and go to work just like always. We go to the same restaurant, just like always. We do so many things over and over that it can be challenging to notice that any progress is actually happening. An even more troublesome thought is that God gave you a big vision and nothing you see looks remotely like it. You live righteously. You tithe and strive to stay surrendered to God's will but nothing looks any better than it did yesterday. Times may but not be changing but you can be confident that you are. You are progressing because it is promised to you by the word of God(**Philippians 1:6**). God who began a good work in you will indeed finish it.In all honesty, it won't look like you are progressing. How do measure the distance when you walk by faith and not by sight?

Walking by faith doesn't have a timeline. There aren't any milestones that you can track or gauge how well you are doing. The walking by faith part isn't easy either.The path can be dangerous. You could literally be walking through a valley of shadow of death and your faith might be at an all-time low because of it. Take heart! The valleys are a sign of progress and so are the highs and lows of faith. Every test is a step in the progression of faith(**1 Peter 1:7**).

There are a few actions that can aid in our journey to progress. One is forgetting the past and the second is reaching forward. Forgetting and reaching cultivate the press that leads to progress. Forgetting things is not new. Can you remember what shirt you wore last year on this date? See we can't remember everything and it's a good thing. God forgets too. He tosses all of our transgressions into the sea of forgetfulness when we repent(**Micah 7:19**). We have to learn to do the same. Certain memories of our past carry a weight that slows us down. We can't press because we are stuck in the past. We have to cast those cares on God (**1 Peter 5:7**) and forget about them.

Reaching is just as important as forgetting. Life can be numbing to the point that we don't pursue anything. We become dull as a way of protecting ourselves from pain. Too bad that this method dulls everything, even the good parts. A heart that reaches needs a fresh yes. You have to pursue the mark of the high calling with a renewed mind(**Romans 12:2**) and heart after God. You might feel like nothing matters but press onward anyhow. The press is not in vain(**1 Corinthians 15:58**). There is a prize ahead of you just waiting for your arrival.

PRESS EQUALS PROGRESS

What are some things that you need to forget?

EVERY TEST IS A STEP IN THE PROGRESSION OF FAITH

List 3 actions that require a press from you.

PRAYER ACTION PLAN

SCRIPTURE: **DATE:**

PRAYER CHANGES EVERYTHING INCLUDING YOU

PRAYER LIST	PRAISE LIST
☐	☐
☐	☐
☐	☐
☐	☐

PRAYER AND REFLECTION

FAITH
ACTION PLAN

WHAT MOUNTAIN ARE WE MOVING TODAY?

RESOURCES

OBSTACLES

WHAT DOES IT PROFIT, MY BRETHREN, IF SOMEONE SAYS HE HAS FAITH BUT DOES NOT HAVE WORKS? JAMES 2:14 (NKJV)

TO-DAY LIST
- [ ]
- [ ]
- [ ]
- [ ]
- [ ]
- [ ]
- [ ]

ACTIONABLE STEPS
1.
2.
3.
4.
5.
6.
7.

THOUGHTS & IDEAS

JOURNAL YOUR HEART

Cast your burden on the Lord, And He shall sustain you;
He shall never permit the righteous to be moved.
Psalm 55:22 (NKJV)

CAST YOUR CARE

JOURNAL YOUR FAITH

"Thus speaks the Lord God of Israel, saying: 'Write in a book for yourself all the words that I have spoken to you.
Jeremiah 30:2 (NKJV)

ENCOURAGE YOURSELF

END-OF-THE-DAY
RECAP & REVIEW

What are your thankful for today?

What battles did you win today?

What lessons did you learn today?

**AND WE KNOW THAT ALL THINGS WORK TOGETHER FOR GOOD TO THOSE WHO LOVE GOD, TO THOSE WHO ARE THE CALLED ACCORDING TO HIS PURPOSE.
ROMANS 8:28 (NKJV)**

What did God say to you today?

I AM
rooted and built up
ESTABLISHED IN THE FAITH
and overflowing with
GRATITUDE

≡ **COLOSSIANS 2:7** ≡

TAKE THOUGHTS CAPTIVE

2 CORINTHIANS 10:5

TAKE THOUGHTS CAPTIVE

2 Corinthians 10:5 (AMP)
We are destroying sophisticated arguments and every exalted and proud thing that sets itself up against the [true] knowledge of God, and we are taking every thought and purpose captive to the obedience of Christ

Philippians 4:8 (AMP)
Finally, [a]believers, whatever is true, whatever is honorable and worthy of respect, whatever is right and confirmed by God's word, whatever is pure and wholesome, whatever is lovely and brings peace, whatever is admirable and of good repute; if there is any excellence, if there is anything worthy of praise, think continually on these things [center your mind on them, and implant them in your heart]

TAKE IT CAPTIVE BEFORE IT CONQUERS YOU.

If the enemy could only choose one area to attack, it's the mind. The mind is the very seat of you. It holds the entrance and the keys to any place you want to go in reality or in your imagination. The mind can derive anything it wants. It can create whatever it dwells upon. Solutions, innovation, and inventions all start with one thought. A singular focus. A critical, inciting spark that releases a wave of ideas that flood hidden spaces in your memory and pour outward into your reality. One thought can break or build. Wars have waged, lives have been lost all over one simple, yet controlling thought. Just one thought is enough to change your entire existence. There is a strong, resonating power in a thought and that is the very reason why it must be controlled.

In the beginning, God created man in His image. This image came with certain traits, one of which is the power to create. God said" Let there be light" and it was light(**Genesis 1:3**). The same trait was given to us, His children. We have the awesome power to decree something and it will be made evident. **Proverbs 18:21** says, "**Death and life are in the power of the tongue, And those who love it will eat its fruit**(NKJV). The course of our life comes from what we say and what we say starts with one thought. This is why we must be vigilant to protect it. We cannot allow even one negative perishing thought to inhabit our mind. It's that serious. What you think shapes what you believe and what you believe determines how you act. Whether proud or simple, a thought that sets itself against the truth of God's word cannot stand. It has to be made captive. It has to be caught, seized, and disrupted. Damaging thoughts can't be allowed to take root in the fertile soil of your mind.

You are what you think you are. If you think you are small then you will be small. If you think you are great then you will be great. What you think matters so think thing good thoughts. Use your mind to imagine good and to focus on what is beautiful about your life. Focus on what is actually true. (**Philippians 4**)Continually consider what makes you hopeful, grateful, and joyous. Dwell on things that bring you peace. Imagination is not just for children. It's a tool that you can use to shape your perception. Use it and use it well. If a negative thought enters in, rudely show it the exit. Take it captive before it conquers you.

TAKE THOUGHTS CAPTIVE

What negative thoughts have you allowed to overstay their welcome?

YOU ARE WHAT YOU THINK YOU ARE.

List 7 positive thoughts.
(Refer to this list when you battle negative thoughts)

PRAYER ACTION PLAN

SCRIPTURE: **DATE:**

PRAYER STRENGTHENS YOU

PRAYER LIST
- [ ]
- [ ]
- [ ]
- [ ]

PRAISE LIST
- [ ]
- [ ]
- [ ]
- [ ]

PRAYER AND REFLECTION

FAITH
ACTION PLAN

WHAT MOUNTAIN ARE WE MOVING TODAY?

RESOURCES

OBSTACLES

WHAT DOES IT PROFIT, MY BRETHREN, IF SOMEONE SAYS HE HAS FAITH BUT DOES NOT HAVE WORKS? JAMES 2:14 (NKJV)

TO-DAY LIST

- [ ]
- [ ]
- [ ]
- [ ]
- [ ]
- [ ]
- [ ]

ACTIONABLE STEPS

1.
2.
3.
4.
5.
6.
7.

THOUGHTS & IDEAS

JOURNAL YOUR HEART

Cast your burden on the Lord, And He shall sustain you;
He shall never permit the righteous to be moved.
Psalm 55:22 (NKJV)

CAST YOUR CARE

JOURNAL YOUR FAITH

"Thus speaks the Lord God of Israel, saying: 'Write in a book for yourself all the words that I have spoken to you.
Jeremiah 30:2 (NKJV)

ENCOURAGE YOURSELF

END-OF-THE-DAY RECAP & REVIEW

What are your thankful for today?

What battles did you win today?

What lessons did you learn today?

**AND WE KNOW THAT ALL THINGS WORK TOGETHER FOR GOOD TO THOSE WHO LOVE GOD, TO THOSE WHO ARE THE CALLED ACCORDING TO HIS PURPOSE.
ROMANS 8:28 (NKJV)**

What did God say to you today?

GO
BE
GREAT

MATTHEW 20:26

GO
BE GREAT

Matthew 20:26 (NKJV)
Yet it shall not be so among you; but whoever desires to become great among you, let him be your servant.

Colossians 3:23-24 (NKJV)
And whatever you do, do it heartily, as to the Lord and not to men, knowing that from the Lord you will receive the reward of the inheritance; for you serve the Lord Christ.

CAN YOU HANDLE BEING GREAT?

Have you ever felt like you were destined for greatness? You should. You were bought with a price(**1 Corinthians 6:20**). You have overcame everything that tried to overcome you. If the enemy had his way, you would have lost your life in the womb. He does not celebrate you, God does. Angels rejoiced when you came to the kingdom(**Luke 15:10**). So as you can see, it's a big deal that you are under Christ's Lordship. You have been given certain rights and you are more than welcome to become as great as you want to be. You have full permission. You are the light(**Matthew 5:14**). Shine it! Do everything you were destined to do. Don't take no for an answer. Be Bold. Be Brilliant. You are a new creature and that creature has no choice but to be awesome(**2 Corinthians 5:17**). Have you accepted all that? Good! Now go serve.

The world qualifies greatness as having a huge bank account, huge house, and a full staff including personal trainer, chef, and maid. These attributes are nice but they don't automatically mean that someone is great. In the kingdom, Greatness means that you are the best servant. To serve means to put other's needs ahead of your own. Being great means sacrifice and loving the unlovable. It means being willing to reach down and pull others out of darkness. It means being able to say no when it hurts and yes when it's inconvenient. Are you really ready to be great?

Let's clear one thing up. Being a servant does not equal poverty. Living a low life and calling it sanctified is called false humility. God didn't add those limits but you most certainly can. It's your choice. Conversely, you cannot and should not set your heart on gaining wealth. You can't serve two masters(**Matthew 6:24**). If your only aim is to get stupid rich just know that you have also aimed to get stupid far from God. There are levels to this and you are called to be content on all of them.

Can you handle being great? You serve a limitless God. There is absolutely nothing He can't do. Go be great! It's already in you. You were made to pray and slay. Don't fade into the background. Don't keep quiet. Shine your light and don't fear what it attracts. God has promised that He will be with you wherever you go (**Joshua 1:9**). So, go! Get out there! You have nothing to lose and everything to gain. Serve at your greatest capacity in whatever God called you to do. Pastor if God called you to it. Start a business. Mop a floor. Write a book. Go on a mission trip. Apply for that Job. Whatever you do, do it for God. Whether you're scrubbing toilets or flying on private jets. Do it unto the Lord. He called you out of the dark into His marvelous light (**1 Peter 2:9**). You don't have to be unsatisfied or afraid. God didn't call the qualified. He qualifies the called (**Romans 8:30**).

GO
BE GREAT

What's stopping you from achieving greatness?

THERE ARE LEVELS TO THIS AND YOU ARE CALLED TO BE CONTENT ON ALL OF THEM.

What has God qualified you to do?

PRAYER
ACTION PLAN

SCRIPTURE: **DATE:**

PRAYER CHANGES EVERYTHING INCLUDING YOU

PRAYER LIST   **PRAISE LIST**

- [ ]
- [ ]
- [ ]
- [ ]

- [ ]
- [ ]
- [ ]
- [ ]

PRAYER AND REFLECTION

FAITH
ACTION PLAN

WHAT MOUNTAIN ARE WE MOVING TODAY?

RESOURCES

OBSTACLES

WHAT DOES IT PROFIT, MY BRETHREN, IF SOMEONE SAYS HE HAS FAITH BUT DOES NOT HAVE WORKS? JAMES 2:14 (NKJV)

TO-DAY LIST

- [ ]
- [ ]
- [ ]
- [ ]
- [ ]
- [ ]
- [ ]

ACTIONABLE STEPS

1.
2.
3.
4.
5.
6.
7.

THOUGHTS & IDEAS

JOURNAL YOUR HEART

Cast your burden on the Lord, And He shall sustain you;
He shall never permit the righteous to be moved.
Psalm 55:22 (NKJV)

CAST YOUR CARE

JOURNAL
YOUR FAITH

"Thus speaks the Lord God of Israel, saying: 'Write in a book for yourself all the words that I have spoken to you.
Jeremiah 30:2 (NKJV)

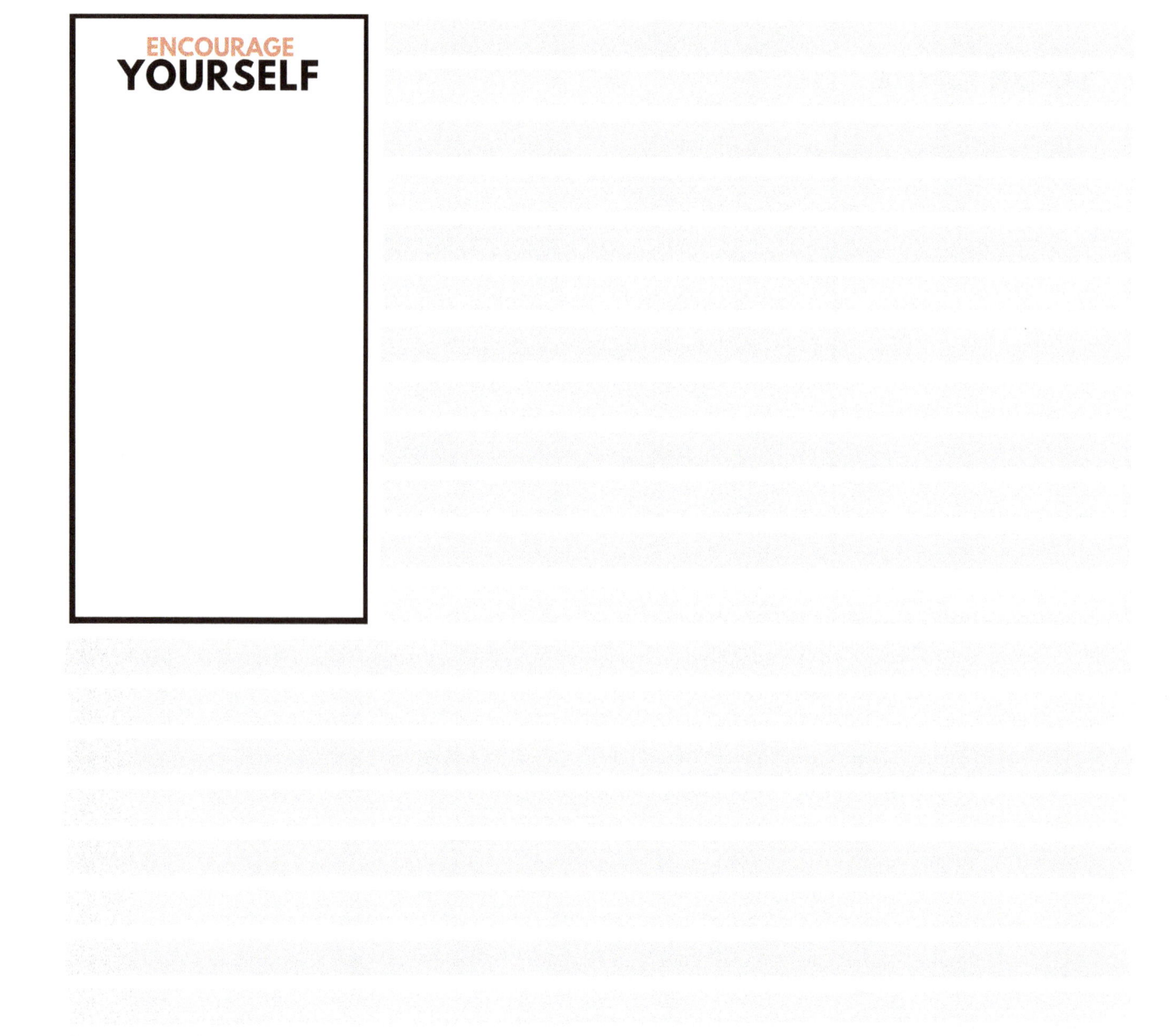

ENCOURAGE YOURSELF

END-OF-THE-DAY
RECAP & REVIEW

What are your thankful for today?

What battles did you win today?

What lessons did you learn today?

**AND WE KNOW THAT ALL THINGS WORK TOGETHER FOR GOOD TO THOSE WHO LOVE GOD, TO THOSE WHO ARE THE CALLED ACCORDING TO HIS PURPOSE.
ROMANS 8:28 (NKJV)**

What did God say to you today?

STOP WASTING TIME

PSALM 39:4-5

STOP WASTING TIME

Luke 10:42(AMP)
but only one thing is necessary, for Mary has chosen the good part [that which is to her advantage], which will not be taken away from her."

Psalm 39:4-5 (AMP)
"Lord, let me know my [life's] end
And [to appreciate] the extent of my days;
Let me know how frail I am [how transient is my stay here].
"Behold, You have made my days as [short as] hand widths,
And my lifetime is as nothing in Your sight.
Surely every man at his best is a mere breath [a wisp of smoke, a vapor that vanishes]! Selah.

MAKE EVERY MOMENT MATTER

87600 hours equal the span of 10 years. There are 525600 minutes in just one year. What have you been doing with all that time? Sorry, not sorry to burst your bubble, but your busyness is not the best part. You are far too concerned about getting useless things done that you miss what is right under your nose. The answer to your prayers, the game-changer, the life-giving beauty of today has been presented to you and you missed it.

Stop moving. Stop doing just for a second and look around you. Look what God has already done. Look at the promises that He has already brought forth in your life. Gaze at the beauty that has graced your family and your friends. Just take a moment. Enjoy the best part. Jesus came so that you can have life and have life more abundantly(**John 10:10**). He gave himself as a living sacrifice so that you could have a better life(**Ephesians 5:2**). He paid a high cost for you to be free from sin. Don't misuse the privilege of the time He gave you. Some people have already met their end today but it is not so for you. Live your life to the fullest.

Use your time better. Make every moment matter. Breathe the fresh air. Take a walk. Pray at the park. Do something that matters to you. If you're unsatisfied with your life then change it. Boldly pursue your purpose. Take a leap of faith. Move out of your comfort zone. Love God and yourself enough to try something different. Think about this for a second: What if you knew this was the last 24 hours of your life? How would your actions change? Where would you put your energy if this day were the last? Time would become precious to you. You wouldn't waste it on pursuing things that don't matter. You would spend your time where it will be the most valuable. So what's stopping you from doing that now?

Our life is but a vapor. It's here today and gone tomorrow. Nobody is going to live forever and that means that today is the best day that you will ever have. Pursue God. Seek Him and let Him add everything else to you (**Matthew 6:33**). Don't waste any more time. There is no need to chase what is already meant for you. Use every second of today to pursue only the best parts. There will never be a better time than the present.

STOP
WASTING TIME

What are some ways that you waste time?

THERE WILL NEVER BE A BETTER TIME THAN THE PRESENT.

What would you do if you had only 48 hours to live?

PRAYER
ACTION PLAN

SCRIPTURE: **DATE:**

PRAYER STRENGTHENS YOU

PRAYER LIST

- [ ]
- [ ]
- [ ]
- [ ]

PRAISE LIST

- [ ]
- [ ]
- [ ]
- [ ]

PRAYER AND REFLECTION

FAITH
ACTION PLAN

WHAT MOUNTAIN ARE WE MOVING TODAY?

RESOURCES

OBSTACLES

WHAT DOES IT PROFIT, MY BRETHREN, IF SOMEONE SAYS HE HAS FAITH BUT DOES NOT HAVE WORKS? JAMES 2:14 (NKJV)

TO-DAY LIST

- [ ]
- [ ]
- [ ]
- [ ]
- [ ]
- [ ]
- [ ]

ACTIONABLE STEPS

1.
2.
3.
4.
5.
6.
7.

THOUGHTS & IDEAS

JOURNAL YOUR HEART

Cast your burden on the Lord, And He shall sustain you;
He shall never permit the righteous to be moved.
Psalm 55:22 (NKJV)

CAST YOUR CARE

JOURNAL
YOUR FAITH

"Thus speaks the Lord God of Israel, saying: 'Write in a book for yourself all the words that I have spoken to you.
Jeremiah 30:2 (NKJV)

ENCOURAGE
YOURSELF

END-OF-THE-DAY
RECAP & REVIEW

What are your thankful for today?

What battles did you win today?

What lessons did you learn today?

**AND WE KNOW THAT ALL THINGS WORK TOGETHER FOR GOOD TO THOSE WHO LOVE GOD, TO THOSE WHO ARE THE CALLED ACCORDING TO HIS PURPOSE.
ROMANS 8:28 (NKJV)**

What did God say to you today?

BLESSED WHO ENDURE

JAMES 5:11

BLESSED
WHO ENDURE

2 Corinthians 12:7-9 (NKJV)
And lest I should be exalted above measure by the abundance of the revelations, a thorn in the flesh was given to me, a messenger of Satan to buffet me, lest I be exalted above measure. Concerning this thing I pleaded with the Lord three times that it might depart from me. And He said to me, "My grace is sufficient for you, for My strength is made perfect in weakness." Therefore most gladly I will rather boast in my infirmities, that the power of Christ may rest upon me.

James 5:11 (NKJV)
Indeed we count them blessed who endure. You have heard of the perseverance of Job and seen the end intended by the Lord—that the Lord is very compassionate and merciful.

LET YOUR FRUSTRATION FUEL YOU

Most consider it a blessing when you receive a new job or are fruitful in ministry. It is very rare that we would consider it a blessing when you endure. Endure sounds like such a hard word. It doesn't bring pleasant memories when you recall those tough times you endured. Yet, the truth of God's word still stands. It is a blessing when you endure hardship in the kingdom.

Hardship is an indicator of refinement, testing, and growth. It is a tool that the Lord uses to sanctify his people. The issue is that it doesn't feel good. Not even one bit. It hurts. It can also make you feel that God has turned his back on you. Don't honor that feeling. Remember the enemy's intentions are to sift you as wheat. He wants you to believe that God will forsake you and he likes to take advantage of you when you are in your most trying time. God does care, AND He uses tough situations to exemplify that love.

It is in hardship that you can see his protection and guidance. It is in hardship that you are the most effective and humble. Hardship is where you learn all facets of God. **Psalm 119:71** says, **It is good for me that I have been afflicted, That I may learn Your statutes**(AMP). Hardship is good. Endurance is the outcome. It is producing in you what is necessary for your journey. Remember Job from the bible? Job lost absolutely everything and he was a righteous man. He preserved through a lengthy trial and received a bountiful reward (**Job 42:12**). So let me be the first to tell you that you are not going through it all for no reason. You will win but only if you don't quit.

There are other times in our Christian walk that we can't seem to pray our way out of. It might be illness, or financial issues. Whatever it may be you have probably danced, praised, fasted, worshipped, gave, slobbered and everything else and still that mountain remains. It probably doesn't make sense either. Remember that God's grace is sufficient for you. It's a promise that means that you have enough in you to handle it. Enduring is frustrating, but use it to your advantage. Let your frustration fuel you. Let it be an indicator that God wants you to rise to the occasion. Let it power your worship. Allow it to push you into your next level. Don't die in it. Endure until the end.

BLESSED
WHO ENDURE

What have you endured?

IT IS PRODUCING IN YOU WHAT IS NECESSARY FOR YOUR JOURNEY

What have you learned through endurance?

PRAYER
ACTION PLAN

SCRIPTURE: **DATE:**

PRAYER CHANGES EVERYTHING INCLUDING YOU

PRAYER LIST

- [ ]
- [ ]
- [ ]
- [ ]

PRAISE LIST

- [ ]
- [ ]
- [ ]
- [ ]

PRAYER AND REFLECTION

FAITH
ACTION PLAN

WHAT MOUNTAIN ARE WE MOVING TODAY?

RESOURCES

OBSTACLES

WHAT DOES IT PROFIT, MY BRETHREN, IF SOMEONE SAYS HE HAS FAITH BUT DOES NOT HAVE WORKS? JAMES 2:14 (NKJV)

TO-DAY LIST

- [ ]
- [ ]
- [ ]
- [ ]
- [ ]
- [ ]
- [ ]

ACTIONABLE STEPS

1.
2.
3.
4.
5.
6.
7.

THOUGHTS & IDEAS

JOURNAL YOUR HEART

Cast your burden on the Lord, And He shall sustain you;
He shall never permit the righteous to be moved.
Psalm 55:22 (NKJV)

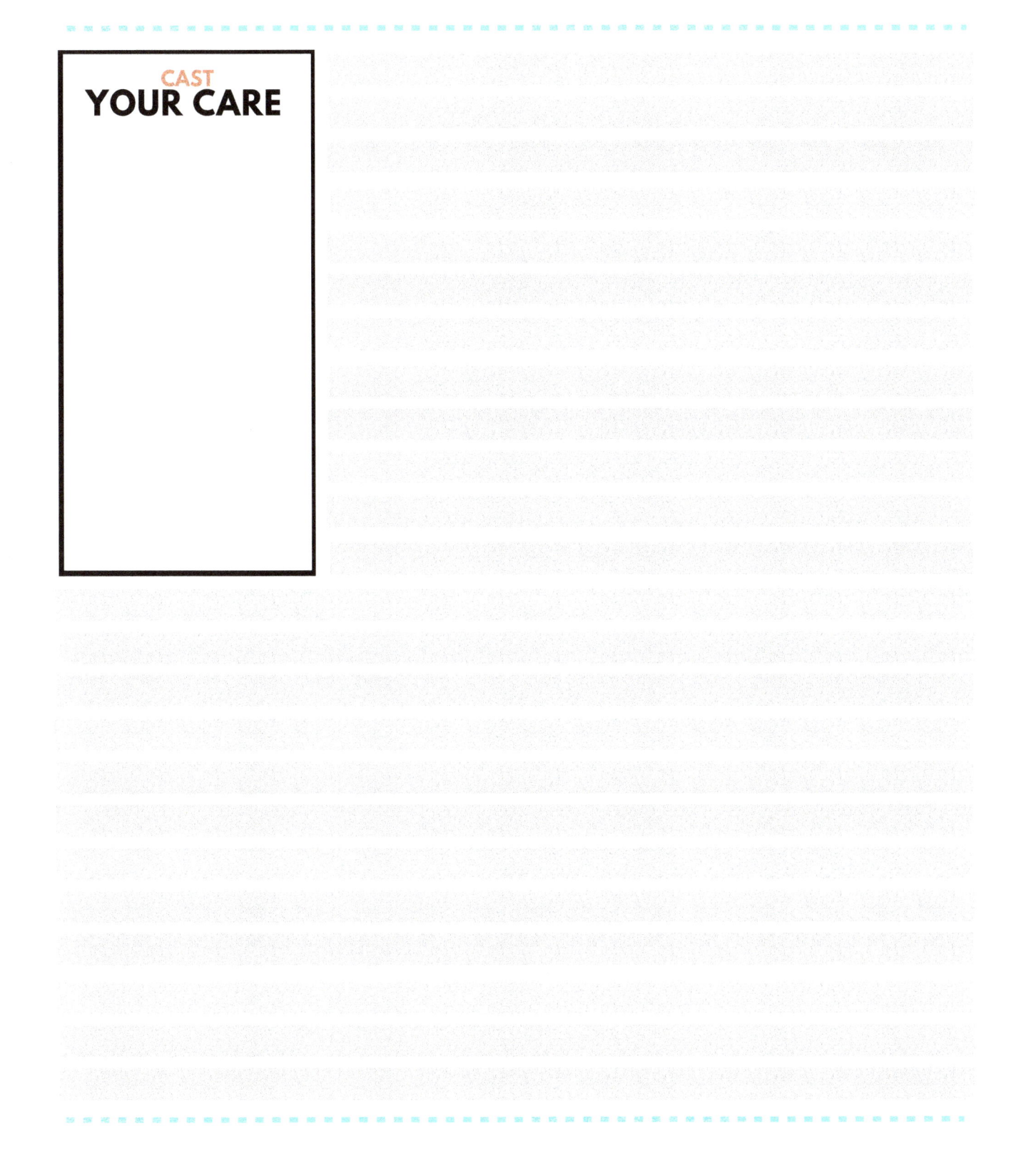

CAST YOUR CARE

JOURNAL YOUR FAITH

"Thus speaks the Lord God of Israel, saying: 'Write in a book for yourself all the words that I have spoken to you.
Jeremiah 30:2 (NKJV)

ENCOURAGE YOURSELF

END-OF-THE-DAY
RECAP & REVIEW

What are your thankful for today?

What battles did you win today?

What lessons did you learn today?

**AND WE KNOW THAT ALL THINGS WORK TOGETHER FOR GOOD TO THOSE WHO LOVE GOD, TO THOSE WHO ARE THE CALLED ACCORDING TO HIS PURPOSE.
ROMANS 8:28 (NKJV)**

What did God say to you today?

I AM
cared for and
SUSTAINED

I will not be
SHAKEN

— PSALM 55:22 —

WAIT

FOR

IT

HABAKKUK 2:3

WAIT FOR IT

Psalm 27:14 (NKJV)
Wait on the Lord; Be of good courage,
And He shall strengthen your heart; Wait, I say, on the Lord!

Habakkuk 2:3 (NKJV)
For the vision is yet for an appointed time; But at the end it will speak, and it will not lie. Though it tarries, wait for it; Because it will surely come, It will not tarry.

THE WAITING PERIOD IS FOR PREPARATION.

Waiting is an expected part of life. You wait at the checkout line at the grocery store. You wait in line at the bank teller. You might even wait in line to get the latest cell phone. It's just something you do when you want something. That same waiting is a fact of life in the kingdom as well. You may request something from God and just like that you're stuck waiting. It may be seconds or months but that action word called 'waiting' is going to happen. You can't escape the waiting period. Impatience doesn't speed anything up but it sure will make you frustrated. Have you ever seen an impatient person in a traffic jam? They weave in an out, from lane to lane to end up at the same spot you are in 10 minutes. You've witnessed it before and it's just unnecessary. Everbody has to wait but the difference between the world and the kingdom is how you do it.

First off, Complaining is a no-no. It is not okay to pray about something then complain. You can designate the prayer but you can't dictate the delivery. How it gets done and when it gets done is on God. Your opinions are nice, but not needed. The God you serve created everything and everyone you see. He made it all from nothing so take a chill pill. He can get it done just fine without your murmuring. He actually despises it as well so it might be best to do yourself a favor and keep your mouth closed(**Numbers 11:1-4**).

Visionaries take heed on this point. The waiting period is for preparation. I know we live in a world where everything is (poof) instantaneous. We want everything yesterday. It's not so when it comes to waiting on God. Imagine you are baking a cake. You have to gather the ingredients. Slowly mix them together in a certain order. Then you put it in the oven and wait a certain amount of time. After about 2 hours, you can sit down and enjoy a delicious home-cooked dessert. It's the same with God. He is preparing things in the background. He is doing things on your behalf and you should be preparing for it. Don't just do nothing. Prepare for what you prayed for! That's what the waiting period is for. It is an action. Serve while you wait. Make room for it. Create a space for it. Prepare your mind for it.

When it comes to God's vision, waiting is a relevant and necessary part of that process. So get ready to wait. Plan to wait. What you are waiting for is on the way. The vision will come to pass, it might take some time, but it will happen. Daniel was a righteous man. Daniel waited. Be like Daniel (**Daniel 10:12**). How will you wait?

WAIT FOR IT

What are some things you are waiting on?

IT IS NOT OKAY TO PRAY ABOUT SOMETHING THEN COMPLAIN.

What have you complained about recently?

PRAYER
ACTION PLAN

SCRIPTURE: **DATE:**

PRAYER STRENGTHENS YOU

PRAYER LIST

- [ ]
- [ ]
- [ ]
- [ ]

PRAISE LIST

- [ ]
- [ ]
- [ ]
- [ ]

PRAYER AND REFLECTION

FAITH
ACTION PLAN

WHAT MOUNTAIN ARE WE MOVING TODAY?

RESOURCES

OBSTACLES

WHAT DOES IT PROFIT, MY BRETHREN, IF SOMEONE SAYS HE HAS FAITH BUT DOES NOT HAVE WORKS? JAMES 2:14 (NKJV)

TO-DAY LIST

- [ ]
- [ ]
- [ ]
- [ ]
- [ ]
- [ ]
- [ ]

ACTIONABLE STEPS

1.
2.
3.
4.
5.
6.
7.

THOUGHTS & IDEAS

JOURNAL
YOUR HEART

Cast your burden on the Lord, And He shall sustain you;
He shall never permit the righteous to be moved.
Psalm 55:22 (NKJV)

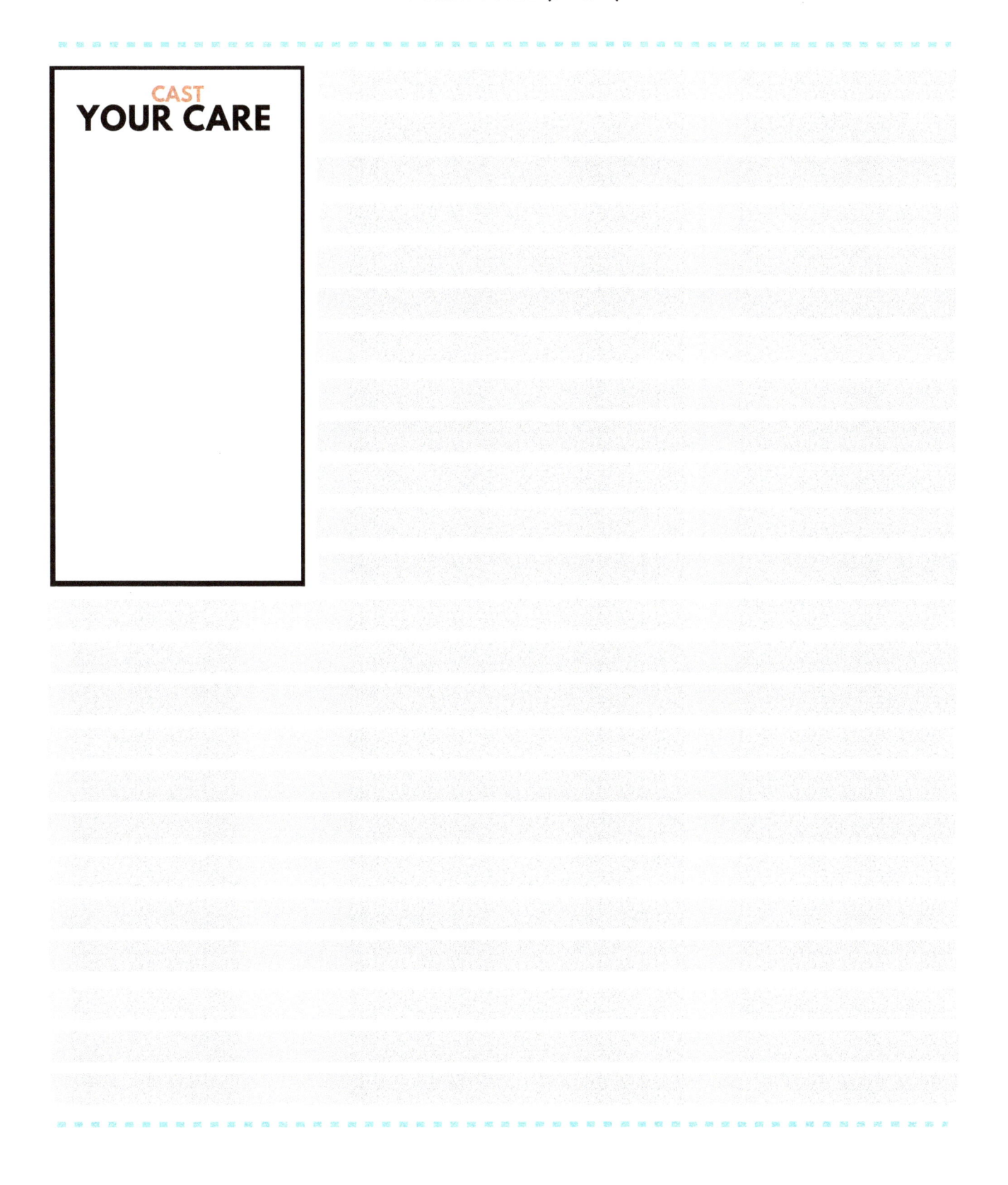

CAST
YOUR CARE

JOURNAL
YOUR FAITH

"Thus speaks the Lord God of Israel, saying: 'Write in a book for yourself all the words that I have spoken to you.
Jeremiah 30:2 (NKJV)

ENCOURAGE YOURSELF

END-OF-THE-DAY
RECAP & REVIEW

What are your thankful for today?

What battles did you win today?

What lessons did you learn today?

AND WE KNOW THAT ALL THINGS WORK TOGETHER FOR GOOD TO THOSE WHO LOVE GOD, TO THOSE WHO ARE THE CALLED ACCORDING TO HIS PURPOSE.
ROMANS 8:28 (NKJV)

What did God say to you today?

DILIGENCE LEADS TO ABUNDANCE

PROVERBS 21:5

DILIGENCE LEADS TO ABUNDANCE

Proverbs 21:5 (AMP)
The plans of the diligent lead surely to abundance and advantage,
But everyone who acts in haste comes surely to poverty.

Proverbs 24:30-34 (AMP)
I went by the field of the lazy man, And by the vineyard of the man lacking understanding and common sense; And, behold, it was all overgrown with thorns, And nettles were covering its surface, And its stone wall was broken down. When I saw, I considered it well; I looked and received instruction. "Yet a little sleep, a little slumber, A little folding of the hands to rest [and daydream]," Then your poverty will come as a robber, And your want like an armed man.

DILIGENT PEOPLE GET THINGS DONE

Do you want to want? Let me ask that again. Do you want to want? It's a simple question with a simple answer. Psalms 23 states that we shall not want. It's not just a sentimental statement. It's God's promise of provision. He supplies what we need but He is not going bring it straight to you. In the context of God as our Sheppard, the sheep lay in green pastures but they have to walk there. They have to go and get the food He provides. They have to go to the water if they want a drink. The sheep have to move so what makes you any different? Why do you think that God is just going to hand it to you? What evidence do you have that supports that God operates that way? The Children of Israel had to fight for the promised land(**Joshua**). Gideon had to fight(**Judges 7**). David had to fight(**2 Samuel 5:17-25**). The woman with the issue of Blood sought after her healing(**Luke 8:43-48**).The blind man called out for healing (**Mark 10:46-52**). Hannah ran into the temple (**1 Samuel 1**). With all these biblical examples of action, what in your mind makes you think that you have no responsibility for your sustainment or success?

Let's break this down a bit further. God gave us the power to get wealth (**Deuteronomy 8:18**). This ability is readily available to you but you have to get up and go get it. Do you want it? or would you rather be lazy? You have to choose one. **Proverbs 13:4** says "**The soul of a lazy man desires, and has nothing; But the soul of the diligent shall be made rich,**"(NKJV). It is not enough to desire something to get done. You have to set about a plan and be steadfast in completing it.

Diligence means you have a plan and actions that follow. It also means that you are intentional about your time. Life doesn't just happen for diligent people. They work. They expect and they execute. Their plans lead to abundance and advantage. Diligent people don't sleep days away.They are disciplined even in their rest and relaxation. They set boundaries. They meet goals. They use their resources. They are faithful with what is given to them. Diligent people get things done. It is the hand of the diligent that will rule , not the lazy (**Proverbs 12:24**).

The gift of the present presents you with two options: Laziness or Diligence. One requires no effort and the other requires everything you've got. If you are ready to live a life full of advantage and abundance then get to work. Repent for being lazy. Get off of your behind. Cut the excuses and put in some work.

DILIGENCE LEADS TO ABUNDANCE

In what ways are you lazy?

DILIGENCE MEANS YOU HAVE A PLAN AND ACTIONS THAT FOLLOW

In what ways are you diligent?

PRAYER ACTION PLAN

SCRIPTURE: **DATE:**

PRAYER CHANGES EVERYTHING INCLUDING YOU

PRAYER LIST

- [ ]
- [ ]
- [ ]
- [ ]

PRAISE LIST

- [ ]
- [ ]
- [ ]
- [ ]

PRAYER AND REFLECTION

FAITH
ACTION PLAN

WHAT MOUNTAIN ARE WE MOVING TODAY?

RESOURCES

OBSTACLES

WHAT DOES IT PROFIT, MY BRETHREN, IF SOMEONE SAYS HE HAS FAITH BUT DOES NOT HAVE WORKS? JAMES 2:14 (NKJV)

TO-DAY LIST

- [ ]
- [ ]
- [ ]
- [ ]
- [ ]
- [ ]
- [ ]

ACTIONABLE STEPS

1.
2.
3.
4.
5.
6.
7.

THOUGHTS & IDEAS

JOURNAL YOUR HEART

Cast your burden on the Lord, And He shall sustain you;
He shall never permit the righteous to be moved.
Psalm 55:22 (NKJV)

CAST YOUR CARE

JOURNAL YOUR FAITH

"Thus speaks the Lord God of Israel, saying: 'Write in a book for yourself all the words that I have spoken to you.
Jeremiah 30:2 (NKJV)

ENCOURAGE YOURSELF

END-OF-THE-DAY
RECAP & REVIEW

What are your thankful for today?

What battles did you win today?

What lessons did you learn today?

**AND WE KNOW THAT ALL THINGS WORK TOGETHER FOR GOOD TO THOSE WHO LOVE GOD, TO THOSE WHO ARE THE CALLED ACCORDING TO HIS PURPOSE.
ROMANS 8:28 (NKJV)**

What did God say to you today?

BE A CHEERFUL GIVER

2 CORINTHIANS 9:7

BE A CHEERFUL GIVER

2 Corinthians 9:7(AMP)
Let each one give [thoughtfully and with purpose] just as he has decided in his heart, not grudgingly or under compulsion, for God loves a cheerful giver [and delights in the one whose heart is in his gift].

Malachi 3:10 (AMP)
Bring all the tithes (the tenth) into the storehouse, so that there may be food in My house, and test Me now in this," says the Lord of hosts, "if I will not open for you the windows of heaven and pour out for you [so great] a blessing until there is no more room to receive it.

ENLARGED TERRITORY REQUIRES RELENTLESS GIVING

God owns everything. All the gold and the silver. The finest and most luxurious commodities belong to Him. He created it all. He freely gives it to his children and if we are to remain Christ-like then we must do the same. The wonderful thing about giving is that it unleashes overflow into your life. If giving can become your mandate, then there will be no way that you can lack. The last statement may have rubbed you the wrong way. You are probably saying to yourself that I have given plenty of times and yet I still lack. This may be true. You may have given but how did you give it?

The bible says that Lord loves a cheerful giver. He enjoys people who enjoy giving to others. Conversely, giving under compulsion, guilt, or even pride will render any gift fruitless. Did it pain you when the church member asked for a 100-dollar offering? Do you tend to give when the atmosphere calls for it? Then don't be surprised when you only receive overflow when the atmosphere calls for it. You will reap what you sow. Sow continuously then you will reap continuously. Sow sparingly then you will reap sparingly (**2 Corinthians 9:6**). It's your choice.

If you have limitations or requirements for sowing, then the same will be for your reaping. Standards on giving only limit you. Enlarged territory requires relentless giving. In Deuteronomy, God is very clear about how He likes his people to act with the resources He provides for them. **Deuteronomy 15:10** says, "**You shall surely give to him, and your heart should not be grieved when you give to him, because for this thing the Lord your God will bless you in all your works and in all to which you put your hand**"(NKJV). You give freely because God gave freely to you. You are to tithe because God gave freely to you.

Whatever your hand seeks to do won't find gain unless the Lord allows it. This means that your house, car, estate, finances and everything that you deem to be valuable is given to you by the Lord. It's not your increase. It's not your vision. It's all His and that's it. You don't own anything. You can invest all you want. You can even go from having 2 cents to being a billionaire overnight. The fact still remains that all you possess came from the Lord. He has given you the power to create wealth(**Deuteronomy 8:18**). He has given you the power to create period. So why must you be so stingy? Why do you hoard what God let you afford?

BE A CHEERFUL GIVER

What are some ways you can be a better giver?

WHY DO YOU HOARD WHAT GOD LET YOU AFFORD?

What is the main thought that prevents you from giving?

PRAYER
ACTION PLAN

SCRIPTURE: **DATE:**

PRAYER STRENGTHENS YOU

PRAYER LIST
- [ ]
- [ ]
- [ ]
- [ ]

PRAISE LIST
- [ ]
- [ ]
- [ ]
- [ ]

PRAYER AND REFLECTION

FAITH
ACTION PLAN

WHAT MOUNTAIN ARE WE MOVING TODAY?

RESOURCES

OBSTACLES

WHAT DOES IT PROFIT, MY BRETHREN, IF SOMEONE SAYS HE HAS FAITH BUT DOES NOT HAVE WORKS? JAMES 2:14 (NKJV)

TO-DAY LIST
- [ ]
- [ ]
- [ ]
- [ ]
- [ ]
- [ ]
- [ ]

ACTIONABLE STEPS
1.
2.
3.
4.
5.
6.
7.

THOUGHTS & IDEAS

JOURNAL
YOUR HEART

Cast your burden on the Lord, And He shall sustain you;
He shall never permit the righteous to be moved.
Psalm 55:22 (NKJV)

CAST YOUR CARE

JOURNAL YOUR FAITH

"Thus speaks the Lord God of Israel, saying: 'Write in a book for yourself all the words that I have spoken to you.
Jeremiah 30:2 (NKJV)

ENCOURAGE YOURSELF

END-OF-THE-DAY
RECAP & REVIEW

What are your thankful for today?

What battles did you win today?

What lessons did you learn today?

AND WE KNOW THAT ALL THINGS WORK TOGETHER FOR GOOD TO THOSE WHO LOVE GOD, TO THOSE WHO ARE THE CALLED ACCORDING TO HIS PURPOSE.
ROMANS 8:28 (NKJV)

What did God say to you today?

ALWAYS GIVE THANKS

1 THESSALONIANS 5:18

ALWAYS GIVE THANKS

1 Thessalonians 5:18 (AMP)
in every situation [no matter what the circumstances] be thankful and continually give thanks to God; for this is the will of God for you in Christ Jesus.

YOU SHOULD BE THANKFUL FOR WHATEVER YOU HAVE

There is one thing that you can do that will shift your life. You've heard it mentioned in grade school and maybe you might say it occasionally to others, but you have yet to realize it's value to God. It's called Thanksgiving. Being thankful will push your life into unprecedented realms. It seems so simple but it's God's will and He loves it. Put it into the context of a friendship. Let's say you got your friend a nice sweater. It wasn't much but you thought that they would like it. You send them a text message and somehow find a way to get it to them. They tell you thank you and you say no problem. Next thing you know you see your friend on Instagram saying #lovemysweater. You go out to dinner with them two weeks later and they show up in the sweater you purchased them. You can see they love what you got them and that they are grateful. They not only showed their thankfulness, but they expressed it in several ways. Their whole attitude says thank you even beyond the words. After seeing this you probably would buy them another sweater, wouldn't you? You might even buy them some shoes or whatever else you can find because you feel so appreciated by their actions. Apply that very same sentiment forward. Look at what God has done for you. Look at the mountains you have climbed with His help and the valleys you've survived. Look at the many things, impossible things, that He has made possible for you. How can you not be thankful?

Your gratitude should pour out of you. You should shout from the rooftops that God has done marvelous things! But you don't. You've been so concerned about what you don't have that you have forgotten about what you do. It's this forgetfulness and lack of gratitude that will keep you stuck in the same place. God does a miraculous thing and you won't even look at it before you complain about something else. Don't you know how blessed you are? There is somebody right now, crying, pleading and slobbering on an altar somewhere for what you already have. They are waiting for a miracle that you've already been given.

Let this be abundantly clear: You should be thankful for whatever you have, in every situation, and circumstance. It's exactly what the word of God says. It is His will for you. It's the truth but it may be hard to get to that level when you have been continuously heartbroken. There's still hope for you. There are a few things that can be implemented when you don't feel like being thankful. The first thing is to remember that everything on earth is God's. Our homes, children, spouses, and jobs don't belong to us. They are bestowed upon us and they can also be taken. In all these things remember that everything is a gift. When you spend time with your family or children remember that somehow God orchestrated that moment. Thankfulness can also be a mental reset. It is a necessary part of prayer because it switches your focus from the bad to good. **Philippians 4** says that we should think on things of good report and thankfulness puts us into this mindset. In that mindset, we can accept God's peace. Be thankful when you're happy or feeling less than stellar. It will shift your mind if you let it.

ALWAYS GIVE THANKS

How do you practice thankfulness?

DON'T YOU KNOW HOW BLESSED YOU ARE?

What are you thankful for?

PRAYER
ACTION PLAN

SCRIPTURE: **DATE:**

PRAYER CHANGES EVERYTHING INCLUDING YOU

PRAYER LIST

- [ ]
- [ ]
- [ ]
- [ ]

PRAISE LIST

- [ ]
- [ ]
- [ ]
- [ ]

PRAYER AND REFLECTION

FAITH
ACTION PLAN

WHAT MOUNTAIN ARE WE MOVING TODAY?

RESOURCES

OBSTACLES

WHAT DOES IT PROFIT, MY BRETHREN, IF SOMEONE SAYS HE HAS FAITH BUT DOES NOT HAVE WORKS? JAMES 2:14 (NKJV)

TO-DAY LIST

- [ ]
- [ ]
- [ ]
- [ ]
- [ ]
- [ ]
- [ ]

ACTIONABLE STEPS

1.
2.
3.
4.
5.
6.
7.

THOUGHTS & IDEAS

JOURNAL YOUR HEART

Cast your burden on the Lord, And He shall sustain you;
He shall never permit the righteous to be moved.
Psalm 55:22 (NKJV)

CAST YOUR CARE

JOURNAL YOUR FAITH

"Thus speaks the Lord God of Israel, saying: 'Write in a book for yourself all the words that I have spoken to you.
Jeremiah 30:2 (NKJV)

ENCOURAGE YOURSELF

END-OF-THE-DAY
RECAP & REVIEW

What are your thankful for today?

What battles did you win today?

What lessons did you learn today?

AND WE KNOW THAT ALL THINGS WORK TOGETHER FOR GOOD TO THOSE WHO LOVE GOD, TO THOSE WHO ARE THE CALLED ACCORDING TO HIS PURPOSE.
ROMANS 8:28 (NKJV)

What did God say to you today?

I AM VICTORIOUS

I AM AN OVERCOMER

≡ 1 JOHN 5:4 ≡

CHOOSE
FRIENDS
WISELY

PROVERBS 12:26

CHOOSE FRIENDS WISELY

Proverbs 12:26 (NKJV)
The righteous choose their friends carefully, but the way of the wicked leads them astray.

Proverbs 18:24 (NKJV)
A man who has friends must himself be friendly, But there is a friend who sticks closer than a brother.

Proverbs 13:20 (NKJV)
He who walks with wise men will be wise, But the companion of fools will be destroyed.

EVERYONE IS NOT DESIGNED TO HANDLE YOU

Everyone wants to be loved and accepted. We want someone who understands us and what better way to have that than through friendship. A close friend knows you. They celebrate you. They encourage you. **Proverbs 17:17 says that friend is built for adversity**. God created friends for support through the hard times. There are few things better than a good friend and there are few worse than a bad one.

There are people sitting in insane asylums, hospital beds, prisons, and the grave all because they choose the wrong friend. I can recall times as a child that my mother would tell me that I couldn't hang out with a certain child. She would be very selective. I never understood why until I got older. Some of the children I felt were so cool were headed to some dangerous places. You are who you are associated with(**1 Corinthians 15:33**). Some of your so-called friends don't really care about you because they haven't even learned to care for themselves. It's not their fault but it will be your problem if you don't learn to disconnect from unhealthy relationships. Some of your so-called friends are really wolves in sheep's clothing and they are just waiting for a convenient moment to devour you. One mistake with a so-called friend could leave you knocking on heaven's door.

Everyone is not designed to handle you. Everyone is not going to the same place that you are going. Some relationships are only for a season. It's not a bad thing if you grow apart from someone. Accept what God is doing in your life and you also must accept the people He brings in and be willing to let go of the ones He takes out.

Choosing a friend can be difficult but there are some biblical indicators that you can follow. Firstly, a good friend gives good advice. It will be nourishing for you(**Proverbs 27:9**). A good friend will forgive quickly. They will not cut you off after one disagreement. A friend will be there for you in difficult times when you are most unlovable and most vulnerable. A good friend will rebuke you (**Proverbs 27:5-6**). They will encourage good behaviors, not corrupt them. They will be closer to you than your own blood relatives. They will be there to pick you up when you fall. Learn to invest in your good friends and learn to separate from those who aren't. Your life depends on it.

CHOOSE
FRIENDS WISELY

What are some qualities of a good friend?

ONE MISTAKE WITH A SO-CALLED FRIEND COULD LEAVE YOU KNOCKING ON HEAVEN'S DOOR.

What are some qualities of a bad friend?

PRAYER
ACTION PLAN

SCRIPTURE: **DATE:**

PRAYER STRENGTHENS YOU

PRAYER LIST	PRAISE LIST
☐	☐
☐	☐
☐	☐
☐	☐

PRAYER AND REFLECTION

FAITH
ACTION PLAN

WHAT MOUNTAIN ARE WE MOVING TODAY?

RESOURCES

OBSTACLES

WHAT DOES IT PROFIT, MY BRETHREN, IF SOMEONE SAYS HE HAS FAITH BUT DOES NOT HAVE WORKS? JAMES 2:14 (NKJV)

TO-DAY LIST

- [ ]
- [ ]
- [ ]
- [ ]
- [ ]
- [ ]
- [ ]

ACTIONABLE STEPS

1.
2.
3.
4.
5.
6.
7.

THOUGHTS & IDEAS

JOURNAL YOUR HEART

Cast your burden on the Lord, And He shall sustain you;
He shall never permit the righteous to be moved.
Psalm 55:22 (NKJV)

CAST YOUR CARE

JOURNAL YOUR FAITH

"Thus speaks the Lord God of Israel, saying: 'Write in a book for yourself all the words that I have spoken to you.
Jeremiah 30:2 (NKJV)

ENCOURAGE YOURSELF

END-OF-THE-DAY
RECAP & REVIEW

What are your thankful for today?

What battles did you win today?

What lessons did you learn today?

**AND WE KNOW THAT ALL THINGS WORK TOGETHER FOR GOOD TO THOSE WHO LOVE GOD, TO THOSE WHO ARE THE CALLED ACCORDING TO HIS PURPOSE.
ROMANS 8:28 (NKJV)**

What did God say to you today?

BY YOUR SPIRIT

ZECHARIAH 4:6

BY YOUR SPIRIT

Zechariah 4:6 (AMP)
Then he said to me, "This [continuous supply of oil] is the word of the Lord to Zerubbabel [prince of Judah], saying, 'Not by might, nor by power, but by My Spirit [of whom the oil is a symbol],' says the Lord of hosts.

Psalm 37:23-24 (AMP)
The steps of a [good and righteous] man are directed and established by the Lord,
And He delights in his way [and blesses his path].
When he falls, he will not be hurled down, Because the Lord is the One who holds his hand and sustains him.

IT SOUNDS IMPOSSIBLE, BUT IT WAS GOD POSSIBLE

There is a big disconnection in the body of Christ over how God operates. Many in the faith have quit or halted the work all because they believe that they aren't equipped to do the work. They receive a word either by prophecy or spirit to do a certain thing and they go about doing it but only for a short while. As soon as opposition and tribulation come because of the word, they quit(**Mark 4:17**). They take the hardship as a sign that they were doing something wrong. This is the wrong approach to doing God's work.

We are vessels. Utensils to God in which He uses to accomplish His will (**2 Corinthians 4:7**). Our prayer of salvation coupled with righteous living gives Him access to do mighty exploits with us. People are raised from the dead. The blind and deaf are healed. We can do many wondrous miracles, some of which the earth has never seen before but it is and will never be us doing them. It is all God. Before Jesus left the earth, He stated that another one was coming that would help us do even greater works than Him. He was referencing the Holy Spirit (**John 16:7-8**). The Holy Spirit is the power of God. He is our comforter, our shield, our strength (**John 14:26**). It is by His spirit and the spirit that His will is accomplished through us. This means that you are not responsible for the results. Hopefully, this takes the pressure off. God is responsible for his own work. He is the only one that can finish it. Our responsibility is to be available to do it.

We have to be like Mary after receiving the word of conceiving a child with having known a man (**Luke 1:38**). It sounds impossible, but it was God possible. It literally means I am possible. The great I am will finish His word, but we have to be present to do the labor. Mary received the word, but she still had to go through the labor and delivery of a baby. Moses had a staff, but He had to travel back to Egypt to use it. David was proclaimed king, but He still had to keep the sheep. Do you see the pattern? God was with all of them AND they still went through pain, tribulations, and testing. Having God does not mean you become exempt from Hardship. Just because you carry God's vision does not mean you will not face opposition. Having God means that your faithfulness will be rewarded and that your obedience won't be fruitless. So be very strong and courageous(**Deuteronomy 31:6**). Do what God told you to do come hell or high water. It will come to pass for those who make it to the end, for God makes all things possible (**Matthew 19:26**).

BY YOUR SPIRIT

What work is God asking you to do?

GOD IS RESPONSIBLE FOR HIS OWN WORK.

What work is God asking you to NOT do?

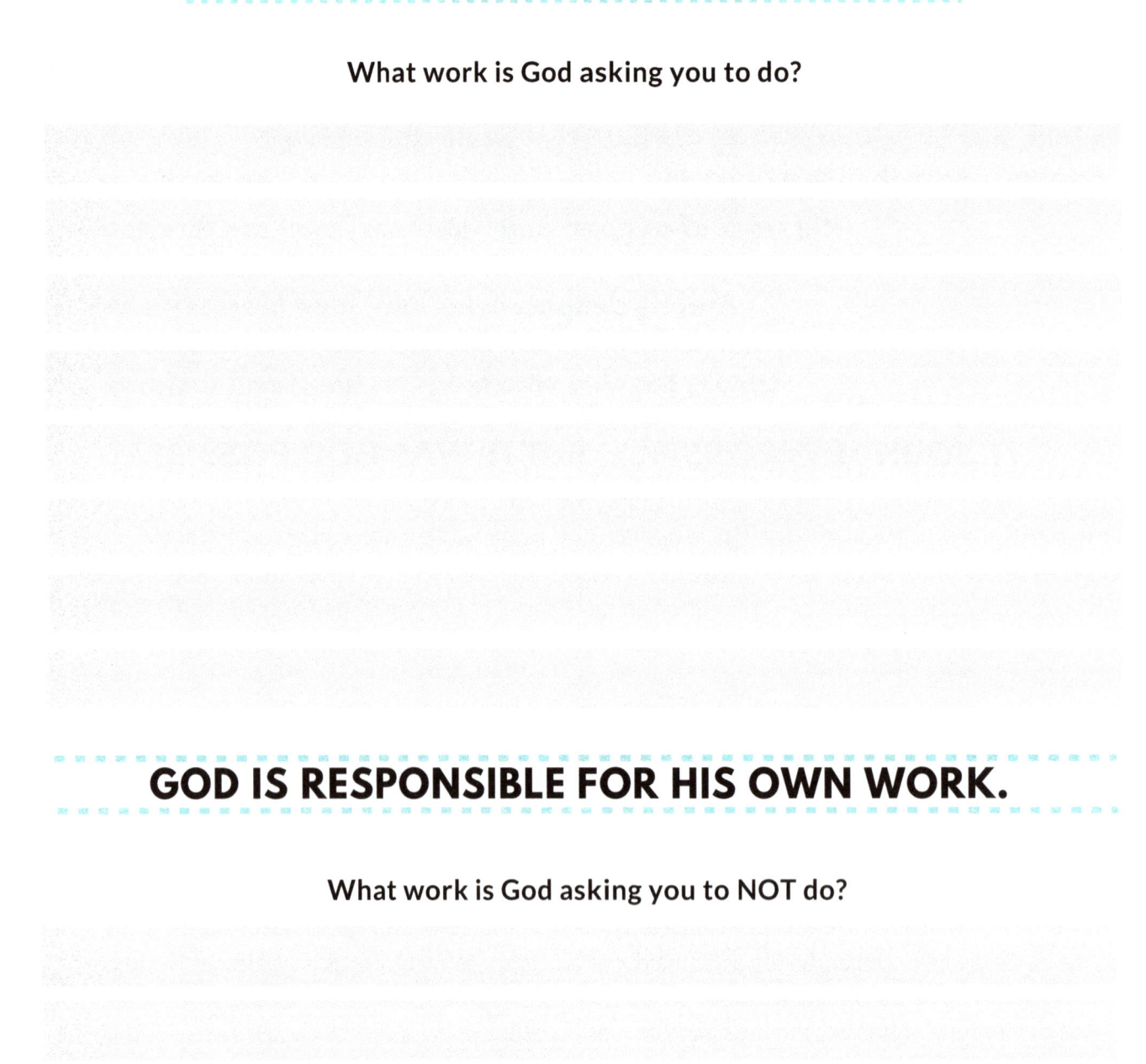

PRAYER
ACTION PLAN

SCRIPTURE: **DATE:**

PRAYER CHANGES EVERYTHING INCLUDING YOU

PRAYER LIST **PRAISE LIST**

☐ ☐
☐ ☐
☐ ☐
☐ ☐

PRAYER AND REFLECTION

FAITH
ACTION PLAN

WHAT MOUNTAIN ARE WE MOVING TODAY?

RESOURCES

OBSTACLES

WHAT DOES IT PROFIT, MY BRETHREN, IF SOMEONE SAYS HE HAS FAITH BUT DOES NOT HAVE WORKS? JAMES 2:14 (NKJV)

TO-DAY LIST

- [ ]
- [ ]
- [ ]
- [ ]
- [ ]
- [ ]
- [ ]

ACTIONABLE STEPS

1.
2.
3.
4.
5.
6.
7.

THOUGHTS & IDEAS

JOURNAL YOUR HEART

Cast your burden on the Lord, And He shall sustain you;
He shall never permit the righteous to be moved.
Psalm 55:22 (NKJV)

CAST YOUR CARE

JOURNAL YOUR FAITH

"Thus speaks the Lord God of Israel, saying: 'Write in a book for yourself all the words that I have spoken to you.
Jeremiah 30:2 (NKJV)

ENCOURAGE YOURSELF

END-OF-THE-DAY
RECAP & REVIEW

What are your thankful for today?

What battles did you win today?

What lessons did you learn today?

AND WE KNOW THAT ALL THINGS WORK TOGETHER FOR GOOD TO THOSE WHO LOVE GOD, TO THOSE WHO ARE THE CALLED ACCORDING TO HIS PURPOSE.
ROMANS 8:28 (NKJV)

What did God say to you today?

THE SPIRIT OF THE LORD
will rest on me.

ISAIAH 11:2

I HAVE THE SPIRIT OF

UNDERSTANDING

COUNSEL AND MIGHT

WISDOM

and the

FEAR OF THE LORD

ISAIAH 11:2

FAITH IS ACTION

JAMES 2:17-18

FAITH IS ACTION

James 2:17-18 (NKJV)
Thus also faith by itself, if it does not have works, is dead. But someone will say, "You have faith, and I have works." Show me your faith without your works, and I will show you my faith by my works.

Hebrews 11:6 (NKJV)
But without faith it is impossible to please Him, for he who comes to God must believe that He is, and that He is a rewarder of those who diligently seek Him.

OBEDIENCE IS WHAT SEPARATES THE FAITHFUL FROM THE FAITHLESS.

You have a vision which is something God gave you. It is a huge vision and quite frankly impossible by your own standards but extremely possible by His. If you were clever you probably have written it down and now you're probably sitting in the corner of your room thinking, "now what?" What in the world am I supposed to do with this? This is the point where religious folks will tell you to wait on God. Don't listen to that. Faith is the substance of things hoped for. Faith is an action word. You must act on the things that you hope for without seeing it. You pray (act) and worship (act) to and for a God that you have never seen. That takes faith. It is the same when it comes to what He tells you. You don't have to know how everything is going to work out. You don't even have to know the whole plan. You just have to be willing to take the first step.

Obedience is what separates the faithful from the faithless. It's that obedience to run after and pursue what you can't see that pleases God. He was pleased when Joshua went(**Joshua 1:5**). Abraham, The father of Faith, went to a land that God spoke to him about without even knowing where it was(**Genesis 12:4**). He believed and that's all he needed. It's the same for you. You don't have to know the plan. You just need to know the plan maker.

Pursue that today. Acknowledge your fears. Then stomp the life out of them with your faith. Show God your faith by your actions. You may feel stupid or inadequate applying for a job you are not qualified for. You may be afraid to write a book or start a business, but don't let that stop you. If Jesus is calling you out onto the water, you better go! Obey the voice of the Lord. Look foolish if need be. Let them laugh in your face. I'm sure they laughed at Noah, too. Nothing matters but the mission that God gave you. Act on it. Do it. Faith by faith and one step at a time.

FAITH IS
ACTION

What limits your actions?

YOU JUST HAVE TO BE WILLING TO TAKE THE FIRST STEP.

What are some steps you can take today?

PRAYER ACTION PLAN

SCRIPTURE: DATE:

PRAYER STRENGTHENS YOU

PRAYER LIST

- [ ]
- [ ]
- [ ]
- [ ]

PRAISE LIST

- [ ]
- [ ]
- [ ]
- [ ]

PRAYER AND REFLECTION

FAITH
ACTION PLAN

WHAT MOUNTAIN ARE WE MOVING TODAY?

RESOURCES

OBSTACLES

WHAT DOES IT PROFIT, MY BRETHREN, IF SOMEONE SAYS HE HAS FAITH BUT DOES NOT HAVE WORKS? JAMES 2:14 (NKJV)

TO-DAY LIST

- [ ]
- [ ]
- [ ]
- [ ]
- [ ]
- [ ]
- [ ]

ACTIONABLE STEPS

1.
2.
3.
4.
5.
6.
7.

THOUGHTS & IDEAS

JOURNAL YOUR HEART

Cast your burden on the Lord, And He shall sustain you;
He shall never permit the righteous to be moved.
Psalm 55:22 (NKJV)

CAST YOUR CARE

JOURNAL YOUR FAITH

"Thus speaks the Lord God of Israel, saying: 'Write in a book for yourself all the words that I have spoken to you.
Jeremiah 30:2 (NKJV)

ENCOURAGE YOURSELF

END-OF-THE-DAY
RECAP & REVIEW

What are your thankful for today?

What battles did you win today?

What lessons did you learn today?

**AND WE KNOW THAT ALL THINGS WORK TOGETHER FOR GOOD TO THOSE WHO LOVE GOD, TO THOSE WHO ARE THE CALLED ACCORDING TO HIS PURPOSE.
ROMANS 8:28 (NKJV)**

What did God say to you today?

NO PRIDE ALLOWED

ZECHARIAH 4:6

NO PRIDE ALLOWED

Romans 12:3 (AMP)
For by the grace [of God] given to me I say to everyone of you not to think more highly of himself [and of his importance and ability] than he ought to think; but to think so as to have sound judgment, as God has apportioned to each a degree of faith [and a purpose designed for service].

2 Chronicles 32:25 (AMP)
But Hezekiah did nothing [for the Lord] in return for the benefit bestowed on him, because his heart had become proud; therefore God's wrath came on him and on Judah and Jerusalem.

HUMBLE YOURSELF AND ASK FOR WHAT YOU NEED

Most of the time, you are the only thing standing in your way. Everything you want and need are beyond you and that damaging mentality you have been carrying. Sorry, not sorry to break this to you, but are not that important. God can still get it done without you. You shouldn't even be alive. It's not your fitness regimen or your holy habits that keep you. God keeps you and if it wasn't for that hedge about you, you would be dead. The car you drive doesn't matter. The home you own or apartment you rent, or shelter you stay in don't matter. The children that you take care of, blood born or not, weren't made by you. They were formed by God in the womb (**Psalm 139:13**). Your looks don't matter. Don't believe me? Check back with me in 50 years and ask me again. Are you living in your reality yet? You might think you got it all together, but you don't. The little measuring stick that you use to compare your life to everyone else's is so small and relatively minuscule when you look at God's unchanging hand. So, tell me again why you can't ask for help when you need it? Tell me again why you don't want to be a "charity case"? Your whole life is a charity case from God! The vision that God placed inside you is far greater than your pride. Get a grip! This is your reality check. That bad attitude has got to go.

Think about the parable of the talents (**Matthew 25:14-30**). Their master left them all with enough according to their strengths. One got one talent, another two and another five. Their master told them to use it while he was away. Low and behold when he came back two servants doubled what they were given. It was all a party until the last servant came to him. He only got one talent, which is all he could handle, and he buried it. He thought he was being smart, but he really was being stupid. His story can and will be your story if you don't change. One thing I want to point out is that these were servants. I know this seems obvious but think about it. They probably weren't educated or financially competent because the last servant didn't think of putting his talent in the bank. They didn't know much, but the other two servants didn't let that stop them. The Bible doesn't elaborate on what they did but I like to think that were resourceful and didn't take no for an answer. They opened their mouths and got what they needed. I'm sure they asked for help. Whatever these servants did, they knew that they were not going to show up empty-handed. Why do you keep showing up empty-handed? Humble yourself and ask for what you need. Communicate. Jump out there. Tap into every resource you have, and don't you ever let your pride leave you empty-handed again.

NO PRIDE ALLOWED

In what ways have you been prideful?

THE VISION THAT GOD PLACED INSIDE YOU IS FAR GREATER THAN YOUR PRIDE.

What can you do today to humble yourself?

PRAYER
ACTION PLAN

SCRIPTURE: DATE:

PRAYER CHANGES EVERYTHING INCLUDING YOU

PRAYER LIST

- [ ]
- [ ]
- [ ]
- [ ]

PRAISE LIST

- [ ]
- [ ]
- [ ]
- [ ]

PRAYER AND REFLECTION

FAITH
ACTION PLAN

WHAT MOUNTAIN ARE WE MOVING TODAY?

RESOURCES

OBSTACLES

WHAT DOES IT PROFIT, MY BRETHREN, IF SOMEONE SAYS HE HAS FAITH BUT DOES NOT HAVE WORKS? JAMES 2:14 (NKJV)

TO-DAY LIST

- [ ]
- [ ]
- [ ]
- [ ]
- [ ]
- [ ]
- [ ]

ACTIONABLE STEPS

1.
2.
3.
4.
5.
6.
7.

THOUGHTS & IDEAS

JOURNAL
YOUR HEART

Cast your burden on the Lord, And He shall sustain you;
He shall never permit the righteous to be moved.
Psalm 55:22 (NKJV)

CAST
YOUR CARE

JOURNAL
YOUR FAITH

"Thus speaks the Lord God of Israel, saying: 'Write in a book for yourself all the words that I have spoken to you.
Jeremiah 30:2 (NKJV)

ENCOURAGE YOURSELF

END-OF-THE-DAY
RECAP & REVIEW

What are your thankful for today?

What battles did you win today?

What lessons did you learn today?

**AND WE KNOW THAT ALL THINGS WORK TOGETHER FOR GOOD TO THOSE WHO LOVE GOD, TO THOSE WHO ARE THE CALLED ACCORDING TO HIS PURPOSE.
ROMANS 8:28 (NKJV)**

What did God say to you today?

HOPE DOESN'T DISAPPOINT

ROMANS 5:3-5

HOPE DOESN'T DISAPPOINT

Romans 5:3-5 (NKJV)
And not only that, but we also glory in tribulations, knowing that tribulation produces perseverance; and perseverance, character; and character, hope. Now hope does not disappoint, because the love of God has been poured out in our hearts by the Holy Spirit who was given to us.

Psalm 130:5 (NKJV)
I wait for the Lord, my soul waits, And in His word I do hope..

IT IS NEVER TOO LATE TO EXPECT GOOD THINGS.

Have you ever seen someone in Christ and wondered how in the world they are still smiling when everything is going wrong? I'm sure you met that person that is happy all the time. Sadness is a rare occurrence for them. They seem to know something that you don't know. They seem to have a secret and I'll let you in on it; it's hope. Hope is the power of faith. It's even in the definition (**Hebrews 11:1**). Without hope, you wouldn't be able to sustain your momentum in pursuing God.

Hope is powerful because it is an expectation of Good. The world is a devastating and chaotic place. It's full of calamity and tragedy. Every day you turn on the news and see something that probably inspires prayer. Furthermore, we have a spiritual enemy that seeks to steal from us, kill us, and destroy everything tied to us(**John 10:10**). How are we able to cope with all that? Once again, it's hope. Hope expects no matter what. It says that tomorrow will be better. It whispers to your worst circumstances and says God will deliver us. It might not be a loud voice in your head, but you hear it. It does not disappoint. It has an unwavering belief in the turnaround. It's the bridge to faith and the building blocks to vision.

Hope is a tool for the those who follow Christ. It can give you confidence in the worst situations. You can be staring death in the face and remain confident enough to say, "I won't die here." Hope always says that there is more for me. It is confident in God. It knows that God is good, and it expects that good to manifest every day. Use this gift. The world wasn't blessed with hope. People are leaving this earth every day because they lack hope. They can't see beyond their problems and they certainly cannot expect a good end. Don't let that happen to you. God is doing miraculous things in your life.

He is fighting for you(**Exodus 14:14**). Don't let your eyes deceive you. Don't let them convince you that God has forgotten about you. His love for you is being poured out on you day by day and second by second. When your hope is in God you will not be put to shame. Just as His word says, you will gain new strength and power. You will walk out of weariness into a winning season. Your tiredness will turn into triumph. Don't be ashamed to hope. Use it to gird up your faith. Tell your problems about your God. It is never too late to expect good things.

HOPE DOESN'T DISAPPOINT

What makes you hopeful?

DON'T BE ASHAMED TO HOPE

What makes you hopeless?

PRAYER
ACTION PLAN

SCRIPTURE: **DATE:**

PRAYER STRENGTHENS YOU

PRAYER LIST   **PRAISE LIST**

- [ ]
- [ ]
- [ ]
- [ ]

PRAYER AND REFLECTION

FAITH
ACTION PLAN

WHAT MOUNTAIN ARE WE MOVING TODAY?

RESOURCES

OBSTACLES

WHAT DOES IT PROFIT, MY BRETHREN, IF SOMEONE SAYS HE HAS FAITH BUT DOES NOT HAVE WORKS? JAMES 2:14 (NKJV)

TO-DAY LIST

- [ ]
- [ ]
- [ ]
- [ ]
- [ ]
- [ ]
- [ ]

ACTIONABLE STEPS

1.
2.
3.
4.
5.
6.
7.

THOUGHTS & IDEAS

JOURNAL YOUR HEART

Cast your burden on the Lord, And He shall sustain you;
He shall never permit the righteous to be moved.
Psalm 55:22 (NKJV)

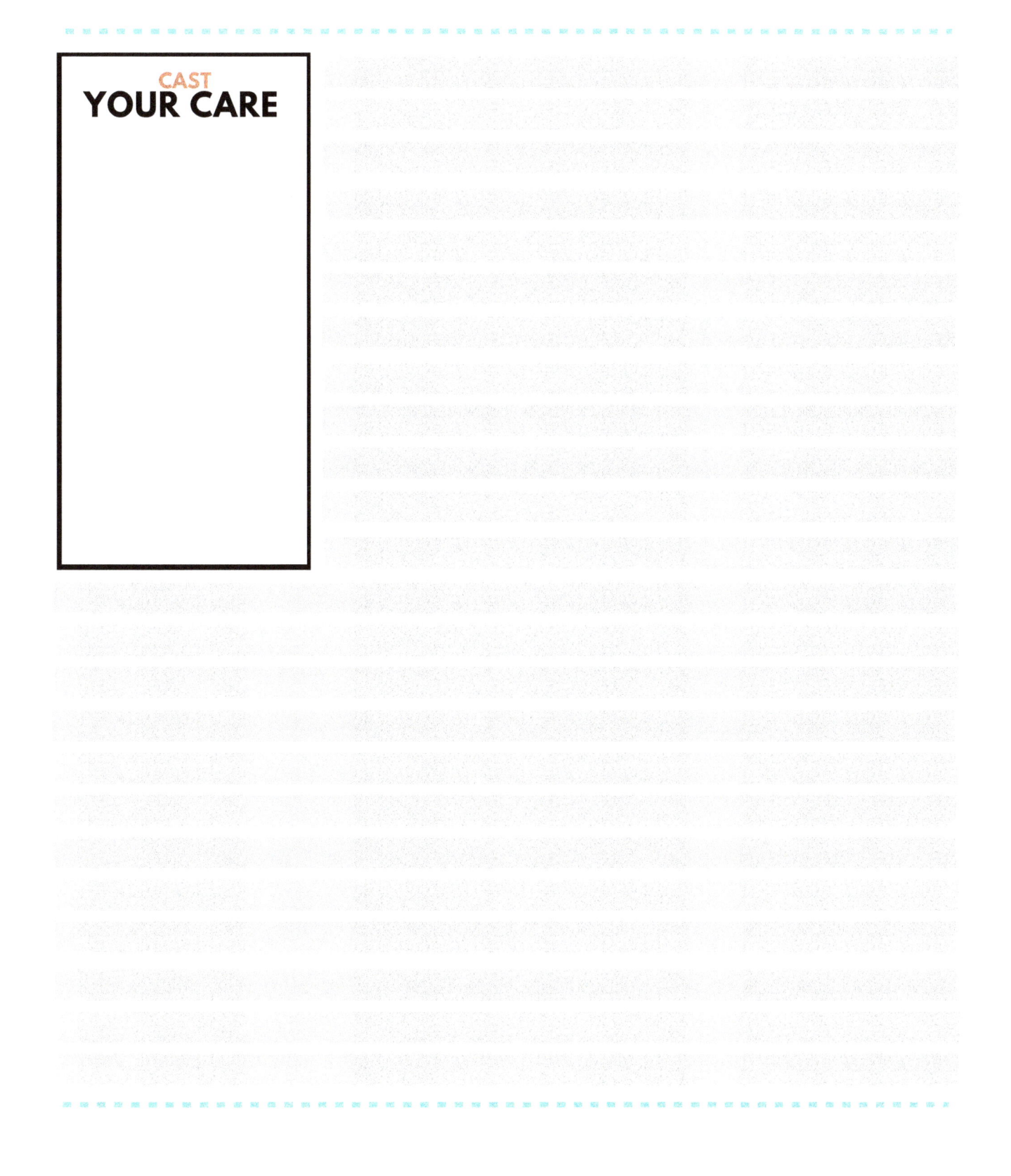

CAST YOUR CARE

JOURNAL YOUR FAITH

"Thus speaks the Lord God of Israel, saying: 'Write in a book for yourself all the words that I have spoken to you.
Jeremiah 30:2 (NKJV)

ENCOURAGE YOURSELF

END-OF-THE-DAY
RECAP & REVIEW

What are your thankful for today?

What battles did you win today?

What lessons did you learn today?

**AND WE KNOW THAT ALL THINGS WORK TOGETHER FOR GOOD TO THOSE WHO LOVE GOD, TO THOSE WHO ARE THE CALLED ACCORDING TO HIS PURPOSE.
ROMANS 8:28 (NKJV)**

What did God say to you today?

THIS IS MY COMFORT

PSALM 119:50

THIS IS MY COMFORT

Psalm 119:50 (AMP)
This is my comfort in my affliction,
That Your word has revived me and given me life.

Joshua 1:9 (AMP)
Have I not commanded you? Be strong and courageous! Do not be terrified or dismayed (intimidated), for the Lord your God is with you wherever you go."

IT IS IN YOUR UNCOMFORTABLE PLACE THAT YOU ARE FORCED TO ELEVATE, GROW, AND MATURE.

Do you know how a diamond is made? It comes from coal that is squeezed with immense pressure. Do you know how you will reach your fullest potential? Under pressure. It might not be from a rock like diamonds, but whatever it is it will most definitely be uncomfortable. God's ways are higher than our ways and He will do everything He said He would, but sometimes those ways don't feel good to us(**Isaiah 55:8-9**). The process of becoming who you are already predestined to be is not a pretty one. If anyone tells you it is RUN, they are lying, and the truth is not in them. God's procedure to process potential is a hard one. He doesn't look at you when you've gotten dressed up or even on your worst day. He looks at your heart (**1 Samuel 16:7**). It tells Him where you need work.

If that's not enough, your holy spirit is communicating to Him with groanings that cannot be uttered (**Romans 8:26**). The whole point is your status, not the cute one you put on social media, but the actual status of your entire being, your soul, is always known to God. It's this report that tells God when to apply pressure and it is fully designed to make you uncomfortable. It is in your uncomfortable place that you are forced to elevate, grow, and mature. David said that it was good that he was afflicted that he might learn God's statutes. The pressure you're feeling is teaching you something. It is forcing you to grow.

Pressure is something that God uses all the time. He uses pressure in the birthing process and with the blood in your body. He uses pressure in deep water and in high altitudes. The deeper you go, the higher you climb, the vision you're carrying, and the vessel you were born in all need pressure. When applied correctly, it will make you strong. Most times we apply it wrong. We take pressure as a sign to give up. We have to learn to continue forward even when we don't feel like it.

We have to learn to press through our pressure to fulfill the purpose over our lives. So, take note of it. Use it to turn you into what God wants you to be. Be strong and very courageous. Don't be afraid to fight through harsh circumstances. Don't crumble under the weight of your own destiny. Let it revive you. Rise up from it and walk into who you are truly meant to be.

THIS IS MY COMFORT

What have you learned from being in uncomfortable places?

DON'T BE AFRAID TO FIGHT THROUGH HARSH CIRCUMSTANCES.

How do you respond to pressure?

PRAYER
ACTION PLAN

SCRIPTURE: **DATE:**

PRAYER CHANGES EVERYTHING INCLUDING YOU

PRAYER LIST

- [ ]
- [ ]
- [ ]
- [ ]

PRAISE LIST

- [ ]
- [ ]
- [ ]
- [ ]

PRAYER AND REFLECTION

FAITH
ACTION PLAN

WHAT MOUNTAIN ARE WE MOVING TODAY?

RESOURCES

OBSTACLES

WHAT DOES IT PROFIT, MY BRETHREN, IF SOMEONE SAYS HE HAS FAITH BUT DOES NOT HAVE WORKS? JAMES 2:14 (NKJV)

TO-DAY LIST

- [ ]
- [ ]
- [ ]
- [ ]
- [ ]
- [ ]
- [ ]

ACTIONABLE STEPS

1.
2.
3.
4.
5.
6.
7.

THOUGHTS & IDEAS

JOURNAL
YOUR HEART

Cast your burden on the Lord, And He shall sustain you;
He shall never permit the righteous to be moved.
Psalm 55:22 (NKJV)

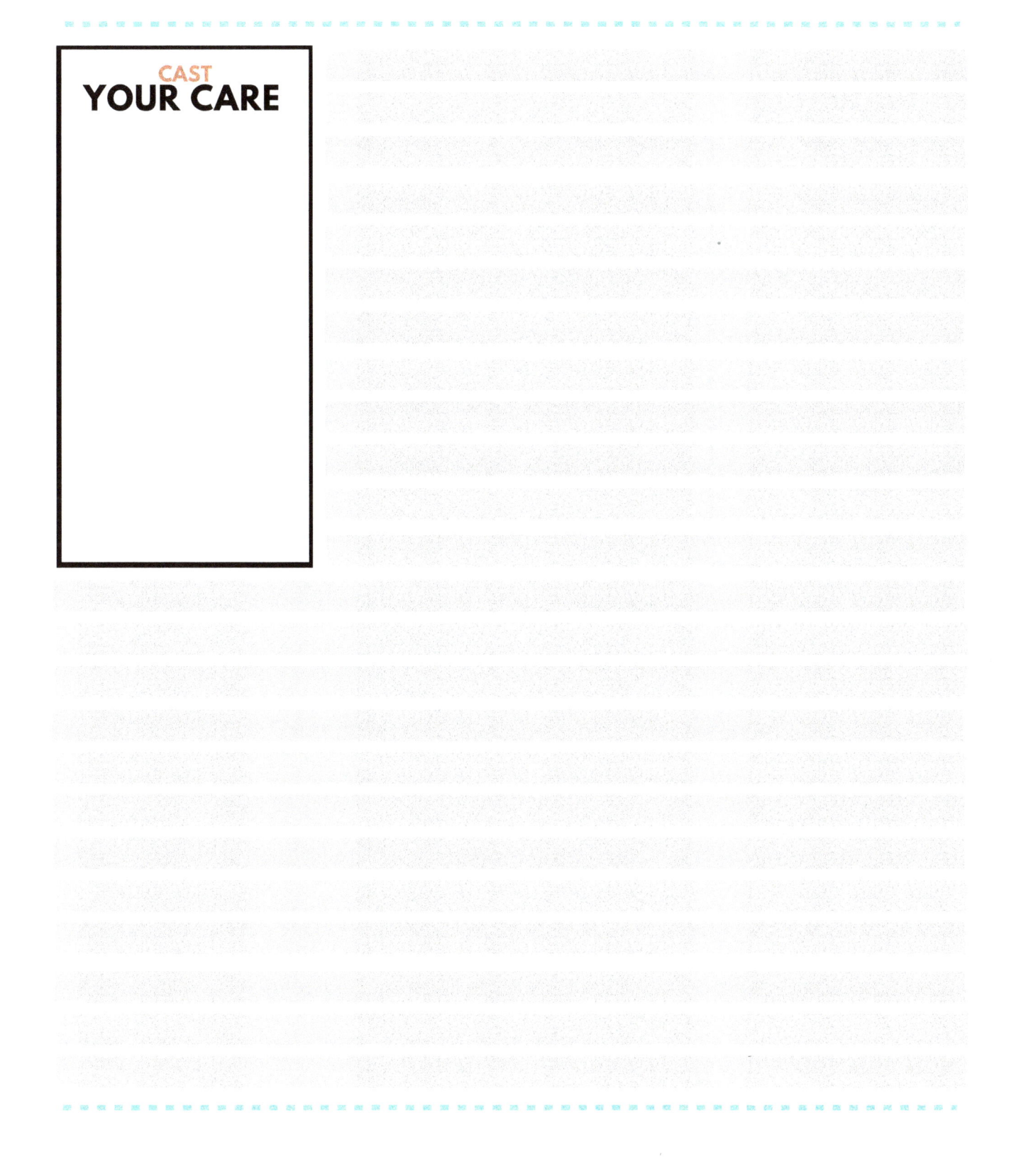

**CAST
YOUR CARE**

JOURNAL
YOUR FAITH

"Thus speaks the Lord God of Israel, saying: 'Write in a book for yourself all the words that I have spoken to you.
Jeremiah 30:2 (NKJV)

ENCOURAGE YOURSELF

END-OF-THE-DAY
RECAP & REVIEW

What are your thankful for today?

What battles did you win today?

What lessons did you learn today?

**AND WE KNOW THAT ALL THINGS WORK TOGETHER FOR GOOD TO THOSE WHO LOVE GOD, TO THOSE WHO ARE THE CALLED ACCORDING TO HIS PURPOSE.
ROMANS 8:28 (NKJV)**

What did God say to you today?

I WILL NOT FEAR because I AM REDEEMED.

God calls me by name.

I AM HIS.

— ISAIAH 43:1 —

TIME TO FISH

MATTHEW 4:18-19

TIME TO FISH

Matthew 4:18-19 (AMP)
As Jesus was walking by the Sea of Galilee, He noticed two brothers, Simon who was called Peter, and Andrew his brother, casting a net into the sea; for they were fishermen. And He said to them, "Follow Me[as My disciples, accepting Me as your Master and Teacher and walking the same path of life that I walk], and I will make you fishers of men."

Mark 16:15 (AMP)
And He said to them, "Go into all the world and preach the gospel to all creation.

THE VERY REASON YOU ARE ALIVE IS TO PROVE TO OTHERS THAT GOD REALLY DOES EXIST

God's vision for your life should line up to one ultimate goal and that's to spread the gospel (**Matthew 28:19**). I know when we hear that phrase we automatically think two things. The first one says that's what the apostles did. Second is spreading the gospel is not for me. While it's true that the apostles heeded the call of Jesus to spread the good news, it is also true that He charged everyday Christians to do the same. So, grab a rod because you are indeed a fisherman.

You were created as a compass that always points to God. The very reason you are alive is to prove to others that God really does exist. It's not always in your words that this happens. Most times people will see God through your life. Religion has unfortunately made this extremely complicated. They have attached 5,000 rules and process to qualify what a fisherman of men looks like. You must be dressed a certain way and you have to attend a certain church for a certain number of Sundays to be able to preach about Jesus. Don't forget that you must have a title and your bank account should be sanctified, too. It can get pretty ridiculous. Be warned. You will most definitely encounter these types of people just as Jesus did. They will try to disqualify you by whatever standard they have made up in their minds and you better believe they will have scriptural references. It still doesn't matter. You have but two requirements to follow and that's to love God and love your neighbor as you would love yourself (**Matthew 22:37**). Nowhere in the scripture did it say be a people-pleaser. Free yourself from that man-made mandate.

God wants you to fish. He wants you to cast down YOUR nets not someone else's. Your net is your testimony. It's all that you have gone through. It is by our testimonies and the blood of the lamb that we overcome(**Revelation 12:11**). There is power in your unique story that can set people free. They need to hear what God has done but more importantly, they need to SEE through your life what a Savior is truly capable of.

TIME TO
FISH

What is your testimony?

HE WANTS YOU TO CAST DOWN YOUR NETS NOT SOMEONE ELSE'S.

What are some ways you can share the gospel?

PRAYER
ACTION PLAN

SCRIPTURE: DATE:

PRAYER STRENGTHENS YOU

PRAYER LIST

- [ ]
- [ ]
- [ ]
- [ ]

PRAISE LIST

- [ ]
- [ ]
- [ ]
- [ ]

PRAYER AND REFLECTION

FAITH
ACTION PLAN

WHAT MOUNTAIN ARE WE MOVING TODAY?

RESOURCES

OBSTACLES

WHAT DOES IT PROFIT, MY BRETHREN, IF SOMEONE SAYS HE HAS FAITH BUT DOES NOT HAVE WORKS? JAMES 2:14 (NKJV)

TO-DAY LIST

- [ ]
- [ ]
- [ ]
- [ ]
- [ ]
- [ ]
- [ ]

ACTIONABLE STEPS

1.
2.
3.
4.
5.
6.
7.

THOUGHTS & IDEAS

JOURNAL YOUR HEART

Cast your burden on the Lord, And He shall sustain you;
He shall never permit the righteous to be moved.
Psalm 55:22 (NKJV)

CAST YOUR CARE

JOURNAL YOUR FAITH

"Thus speaks the Lord God of Israel, saying: 'Write in a book for yourself all the words that I have spoken to you.
Jeremiah 30:2 (NKJV)

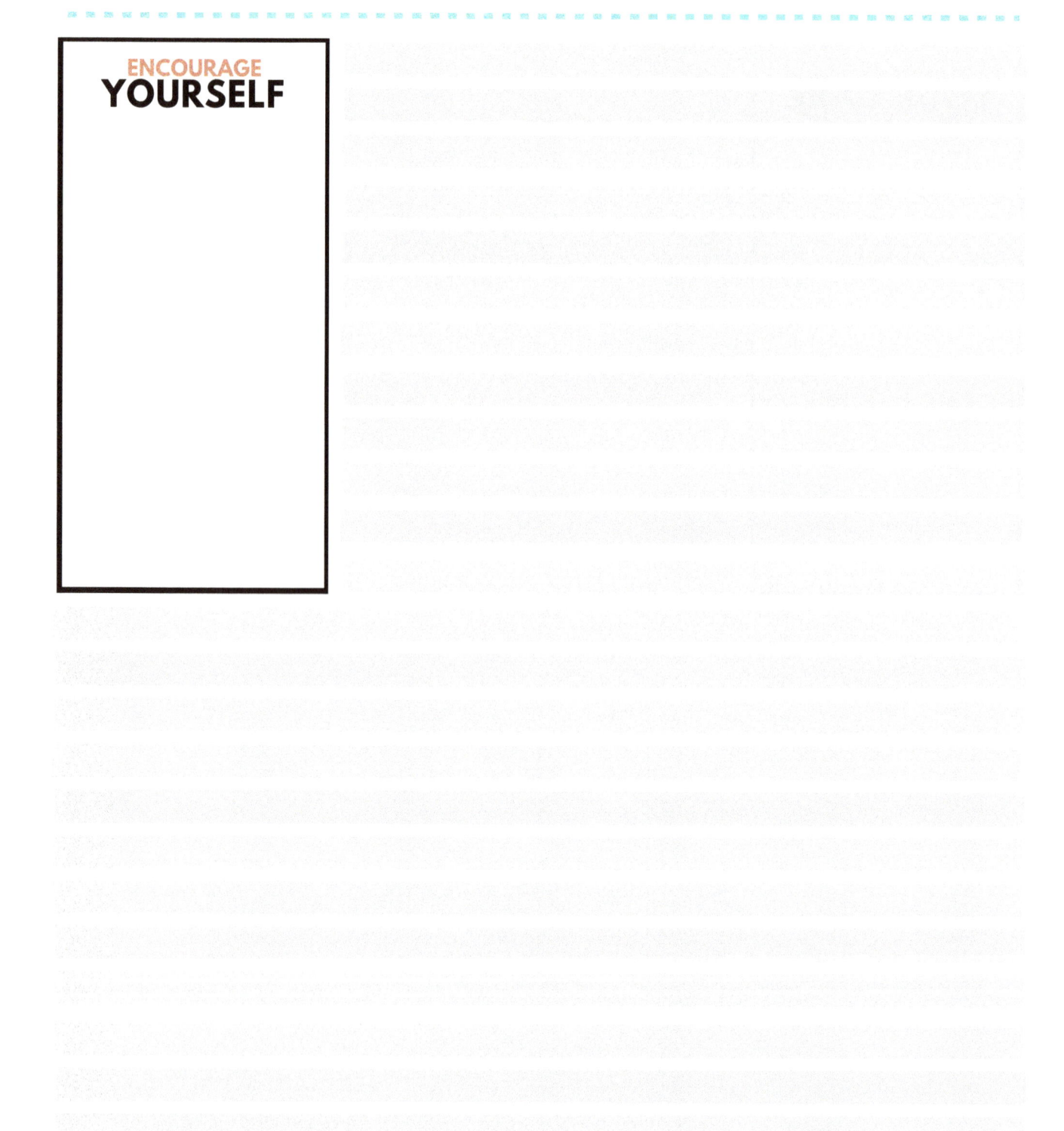

ENCOURAGE YOURSELF

END-OF-THE-DAY
RECAP & REVIEW

What are your thankful for today?

What battles did you win today?

What lessons did you learn today?

**AND WE KNOW THAT ALL THINGS WORK TOGETHER FOR GOOD TO THOSE WHO LOVE GOD, TO THOSE WHO ARE THE CALLED ACCORDING TO HIS PURPOSE.
ROMANS 8:28 (NKJV)**

What did God say to you today?

HALLE LU JAH

REVELATION 19:6

HALLE LUJAH

Revelation 19:6 (AMP)
Then I heard something like the shout of a vast multitude, and like the boom of many pounding waves, and like the roar of mighty peals of thunder, saying, "Hallelujah! For the Lord our God, the Almighty, [the Omnipotent, the Ruler of all] reigns.

Romans 10:9 (AMP)
because if you acknowledge and confess with your mouth that Jesus is Lord [recognizing His power, authority, and majesty as God], and believe in your heart that God raised Him from the dead, you will be saved.

FIND THE STRENGTH TO PART YOUR LIPS WITH ONE WORD: HALLELUJAH.

When all else fails. Say hallelujah. When all goes well say hallelujah. When all your money is spent say hallelujah. When you've barely enough to pay the rent, say hallelujah. Say it quietly over your meal and shout it loud whenever you feel. Give God praise for each and every moment you see. Those that leave you overjoyed and the ones that make you lose speech.

Hallelujah is a powerful word. It is one that can be used when you've had the best day or when you just can't function anymore. It shifts your entire being because it is what you were created to do. You were created to give God praise (**Psalm 66:2**). It is in the very fiber of your DNA. Whatever presents itself to you today should be met with a Hallelujah. Did you pay a bill? Hallelujah. Did you graduate? Hallelujah. Did you gain a new family member? Hallelujah. Did you lose one? Hallelujah. Praise God all the time and every time.

If you get thrown into a fiery furnace like the 3 Hebrew boys (**Daniel 3**). If you get tossed into a pit like Joseph (**Genesis 37:24**). If you lose a close friend like David (**2 Samuel 1**). If you flee from God's will like Jonah(**Jonah 1**). If you get laughed at like Elisha (**2 Kings 2:23**). If you get angry like Peter (**John 18:10**). If you get incarcerated like Paul (**Acts 16:16-40**). If you're forced into poverty like Gideon(**Judges 6:15**). If you are given unimaginable wisdom like Solomon(**1 Kings 3**). If you are healed like Bartimaeus (**Mark 10:46-52**). If you must plead like Hannah (**1 Samuel 1:9-28**).

If you have to repent like the King of Nineveh (**Jonah 3**). If you have to fight like Joshua (**Joshua 10**). If you have to lead like Deborah (**Judges 4**). If you have to flee like Elijah (**1 Kings 19**). If you have to risk your life like Esther (**Esther 5**). If you have to give up what you love most like Abraham (**Genesis 22**). Whatever you do. Whatever you go through. Whatever situation you end up in. Whatever thoughts you battle. Wherever your journey takes you. Find the strength to part your lips with one word: Hallelujah. Glory to God forever and ever. Amen.

HALLELUJAH

Why do you give God praise?

HALLELUJAH IS A POWERFUL WORD

What current circumstance requires a hallelujah from you?

PRAYER
ACTION PLAN

SCRIPTURE: **DATE:**

PRAYER CHANGES EVERYTHING INCLUDING YOU

PRAYER LIST   **PRAISE LIST**

- [ ]
- [ ]
- [ ]
- [ ]

PRAISE LIST

- [ ]
- [ ]
- [ ]
- [ ]

PRAYER AND REFLECTION

FAITH
ACTION PLAN

WHAT MOUNTAIN ARE WE MOVING TODAY?

RESOURCES

OBSTACLES

WHAT DOES IT PROFIT, MY BRETHREN, IF SOMEONE SAYS HE HAS FAITH BUT DOES NOT HAVE WORKS? JAMES 2:14 (NKJV)

TO-DAY LIST
- [ ]
- [ ]
- [ ]
- [ ]
- [ ]
- [ ]
- [ ]

ACTIONABLE STEPS
1.
2.
3.
4.
5.
6.
7.

THOUGHTS & IDEAS

JOURNAL YOUR HEART

Cast your burden on the Lord, And He shall sustain you;
He shall never permit the righteous to be moved.
Psalm 55:22 (NKJV)

CAST YOUR CARE

JOURNAL YOUR FAITH

"Thus speaks the Lord God of Israel, saying: 'Write in a book for yourself all the words that I have spoken to you.
Jeremiah 30:2 (NKJV)

ENCOURAGE YOURSELF

END-OF-THE-DAY
RECAP & REVIEW

What are your thankful for today?

What battles did you win today?

What lessons did you learn today?

**AND WE KNOW THAT ALL THINGS WORK TOGETHER FOR GOOD TO THOSE WHO LOVE GOD, TO THOSE WHO ARE THE CALLED ACCORDING TO HIS PURPOSE.
ROMANS 8:28 (NKJV)**

What did God say to you today?

THE LORD
is my shepherd.

I lack
NOTHING.

═ PSALM 23:1 ═

GOODBYE *Fear*

Fear is paralyzing.
Fear keeps you stuck.
Fear leaves you wandering in circles.
Fear holds you hostage.

IT'S TIME TO PART WAYS WITH FEAR

You weren't made to live in fear. You have a purpose and you can't afford to lose any more days being held back by fear. Visit our website at:

THELIGHTEDLADY.COM/THEBOLDLIFE

To download your FREE copy of THE BOLD LIFE. It's time for you to break the cycle of fear. Learn how to be bold in challenging circumstances. Develop the inner warrior and discover how to walk in freedom without the boundaries of fear.

ABOUT THE AUTHOR

Let me introduce myself. My name is Sasha Le'dawn and I am a writer. Sasha means protector of men and Le'dawn translates to the dawn or sunrise. If we put that all together, I am the protector that always rises. Typically, this is the part where I would list my accomplishments and the 10 million reasons why you should trust what I say but I won't do that. I find it more important for you to know my story. After all, none of that flashy stuff really matters. What truly matters is that I am a real person just like you. I have been abandoned. I have been bruised. I have seen my own visions and dreams crumble to the ground. I've lost all hope and joy. I have experienced traumatic loss and have recovered from the brink of suicide. I SURVIVED BECAUSE OF CHRIST. My hope is to share that victory with you.

I believe that everyone has a purpose and I refuse to believe that anyone is just an afterthought of God. Even in the midst of our darkest pain and deepest fears, God is still loving and good.

WHERE TO FIND ME

thelightedlady.com

Twitter @thelightedlady

Instagram @thelightedlady

Facebook @thelightedlady

Pinterest @thelightedlady

Snapchat @sashaledawn

Instagram @sashaledawn

IMAGE CREDIT: WHITNEY BRE | WHITNEYBRE.COM

CPSIA information can be obtained
at www.ICGtesting.com
Printed in the USA
FSHW01n0930030518
47552FS